Thurs. – Town-Hall – 6.

NEW METHODS
IN THE
SOCIAL STUDIES

NEW METHODS
IN THE
SOCIAL STUDIES

BY

M. J. STORMZAND
PROFESSOR OF EDUCATION
OCCIDENTAL COLLEGE

AND

ROBERT H. LEWIS
DEPARTMENT OF SOCIAL STUDIES
SAN FERNANDO HIGH SCHOOL
LOS ANGELES, CALIFORNIA

NEW YORK
FARRAR & RINEHART, INC.
1935

INTRODUCTION

Changes in content and methods in the social studies are among the most significant elements in the reorganization of secondary education during the last decade. Curriculum revision in history, geography, and civics, and experimentation in the teaching of these subjects, all with the intent of vitalizing them and making them contribute more directly to the socialization of students, have been undertaken in a variety of independent enterprises in many of the progressive educational centers of the country.

Various of these new plans, published in local courses of study or reported in state and national gatherings, have undergone a process of gradual extension into other schools. Some of these programs have been adopted so widely and have met with such approval that they are worthy of consideration and experimentation by teachers of the social studies everywhere.

It is our purpose to present an extended description and explanation of a few of the most widely used and most successful of these plans for the teaching of the social studies. The plans will be presented in a practical way, in comparison and contrast with some of the older, traditional methods. Teachers interested in the improvement of their instruction will be free to adopt or adapt such of the elements of the new schemes as appeal to their judgment.

The principal innovations that are to be discussed are:

The Unit Plan
Workbooks and Study Guide Tests
The Problem Method as Based on Current Events
Socializing Class Methods
Laboratory Methods and Visual Aids
Integration of the Social Studies with English

A chapter will be devoted to each of these movements. Then will follow a chapter evaluating some of the more common traditional practices that involve elements worth conserving. A concluding chapter will be devoted to a consideration of the social studies objectives, showing how these have influenced the modifications of curriculum and methods described in the book.

M. J. S.
R. H. L.

Los Angeles, California
April, 1935

CONTENTS

Meaning of the Unit Plan—Unit-plan Organizations Arbitrary—Illustrations of Unit Outlines—Chronological and Topical Units—Other Interpretations of the Unit Plan

Methods in Unit-plan Instruction: Introducing the Unit—First Reading for Unit Perspective—Evaluating Discussions—Planning Individual Work—Individual Student Activities—Class Activities Under the Unit Plan—Summary of the Unit

Critical Evaluations of Extreme Unit Plans—Correlations in the Unit Plan—Degrees of Correlation—Broader Scope of the Unit Plan Based on Pupil Interests

Bibliography

Evolution of the Workbook Method—The Variety of Workbooks Available—Workbooks Have Subject Point of View

Varying Purposes in Workbooks: For Supplementary Drill —For Self-Testing and Diagnosis—As a Basis for Remedial Instruction—For the Teacher's Testing of Pupils—As Study Guides—As Guides to Collateral Reading

Workbooks Used with New Methods—Not Mere Busywork—In Rural Schools—For Special Classes and Pupils

Bibliography

The Method Explained: Various Forms of the Problem Method—The Meaning of a Problem—Present-day Problems—Students' Personal Social Problems—Supplementary Use of Current Events—The Use of Current Events Illustrated

Sources of Present-day Problems: Sources for the Study of Current Problems—The Use of Newspapers—The News Magazines—The Miniature School Newspaper—The Radio and Current Events—Directing Radio Listening—Movie

CONTENTS

CONTENTS

NEW METHODS
IN THE
SOCIAL STUDIES

CHAPTER I

THE UNIT PLAN

New courses of study and daring experiments with methods in the social studies are the most striking evidences of a professional awakening in the high schools of our country. Teachers of history and civics, as well as some of the other social sciences, are demanding a more efficient achievement in meeting the needs of a rapidly changing social order.

In these subjects, so intimately related to our political and economic life, teachers are beginning to renounce their old allegiance to a specialization based on the conventions of a traditional logic. This spirit of experimentation is expressing itself in a variety of plans, some in new organizations of materials, some in improved methods and devices, some in a combined reorganization of content and technique.

The most widespread of these new teaching enterprises are various unit plans, some of which are already officially organized in city-wide or state-wide courses in the social studies.

Meaning of the unit plan.—The term "unit plan" is used loosely in educational literature to. label various types and degrees of curriculum reconstruction. In general, however, it involves the correlated study of materials dealing with a broad topic or problem, regardless of the school subject in which such materials may, in the past, have been classified by specialists.

Superficial examination of some of the new courses of study organized on the unit plan might lead one to think the units merely involved the rearrangement of familiar

3

subject matter into large blocks of work. The units often appear to be mere substitutes for the familiar textbook divisions of chapters, sections, or topics that were, in the traditional courses, intended to suggest typical lesson assignments for a day's or week's work in the usual recitation manner. In fact, some of the unit-plan courses have achieved little more than such a change of perspective.

Even such simple, arbitrary revisions of outline should, however, achieve more than merely give an intelligent semester-plan outlook in the place of a nearsighted following of textbook subdivisions for daily tasks. As a result of the farsighted perspective by units, the reading or study of such broad assignments may also result in a more sensible emphasis on large movements in history or a regional outlook in geography. It may develop a better comprehension of cause-and-effect relationships and may result in a more wholesome neglect of minor details that deaden the pupil's natural curiosity in the narratives of human adventure and social progress or his interest in the descriptions of political, industrial, and economic activities.

A closer examination of the better unit plans will, moreover, reveal that much more is attempted than an arbitrary reoutlining of a particular subject. The units are not merely large blocks of history or geography or civics. There are evidences, in varying degrees, in different courses of study, that the word "unit" is understood in terms of interests and experiences without regard to the stereotyped logic of "subjects." In short, the better unit-plan courses place a heavy stress on, or display a large freedom in applying, the old idea of correlation.

Varying degrees of combination, of consolidation, especially in the unit-plan courses in the social studies, are boldly outlined under the units of interest or the problem units that constitute the bases of the more advanced plans. Indeed, the terms "social studies" and "social sciences" are rapidly becoming accepted substitutes throughout the country for the old subject terms of history, geography, and civics in junior high schools and of history, civics, sociology, and economics in senior high schools. Even in schools where no correlation or consolidation of these subjects is intended or attempted, the school programs will identify typical traditional textbook courses in these various subjects as Social Science I, II, III, and so on.

Where textbooks are available for such correlated courses, as in the junior high school, the consolidated plan has spread most rapidly. As soon as similar books are available in senior high schools for combined courses in history, civics, sociology, economics, and advanced geography, such correlated courses are certain to be substituted widely for the related traditional subjects, whether the new textbooks are arranged in terms of unit plans or other arbitrary devices for correlation.

Unit-plan organizations arbitrary.—One of the most striking characteristics of unit-plan reorganization, when one compares a number of them, is their great diversity. Few are alike. One might, in fact, venture to say that no two are very similar unless one of them has been strongly influenced by the other. In comparing some of the most striking diversities, we discover at once that many of the unique features of these plans are highly arbitrary, clearly subjective, and often extreme in their unbalanced emphasis of units. This is merely the natural result of pioneer thinking. But textbook authors in any subject are bound to observe more or less conventionally established evaluation of topics. The maker of a unit-plan course of study, whether he be a curriculum supervising expert or a dominant member of a reorganization committee, has the freedom of the innovator and the lure of distinction as an original thinker. It may be that he has the convictions of a reformer with regard to past neglect, or overemphasis, of this topic or that. He may see all the history or the geography or the civics of his country hinging on a single movement or problem, perhaps some item that has been lost in the details of former textbook perspectives.

Illustrations of unit outlines.—We may give some examples here at length, both to illustrate the method by which unit plans may be evolved and to show how the teacher may modify a plan voluntarily adopted for experimentation or prescribed by a supervisor.

A maker of a unit plan in American history might, for example, adopt the famous thesis of one of our leading historians that "the frontier has been the dominant factor in the political development of our country." Such a thesis might result in a survey of our history in such broad units as the following:

> How Europe Found a New Frontier across the Atlantic
>
> The Conflict of the French and English Frontiers
>
> The Spirit of Independence in the English Frontier Revolts
>
> How the Leaders of Aristocratic Capitalism Compromised with the Spirit of the Frontier in the New Constitution
>
> The New Revolt of the Frontier under Jackson
>
> How the Frontier Moved Westward
>
> The Struggle between the North and South for the Trans-Mississippi Frontier
>
> The Pacific Frontier
>
> Our Ventures in Acquiring New Overseas Frontiers
>
> Economic and Industrial Effects of the Disappearance of Our Last Frontier

It may easily be seen how readily such units would lend themselves to introducing generous correlations with geography or civics, to emphasizing the theory of geographic influences on history as well as the importance of industrial and economic factors in our political development.

Or one might agree with another author that the Industrial Revolution is the core of our history. One might see how, in brief, such a point of view might naturally give us three major units:

I. How the Industrial Revolution Began
II. The Development of the Industrial Revolution in the Nineteenth Century
III. Present-day Effects of the Industrial Revolution

It can readily be seen that most of the social and economic movements of our history, as well as civic and geographic facts, can be connected with these general units. They might, then, be used to cover the entire field of social science in the eleventh or twelfth grades of the senior high school. A longer course, too, could be formed for the junior high school, in which the seventh grade would study Unit I, the eighth grade Unit II, and the ninth grade Unit III. Even other departments of school work, art, music, physical education, and English, might adopt the same general units of organization for basic related activities, adjusting their work to fit into such a so-called "core curriculum."

One can also see, for example, how such a broad but arbitrary concept influenced the organization of the social sciences in the junior high schools in Denver, where their Course of Study, one of the most widely known and imitated unit plans, presents the following general outline of units:

Seventh Grade

Unit I. Community Life
Unit II. The Industrial Life of the American People
Unit III. The Interdependence of Modern Industrial Nations
Unit IV. The Changing Agricultural Nations

Eighth Grade

Unit V. The Westward Movement and the Growth of Transportation
Unit VI. The History of the Industrial Revolution
Unit VII. The Growth of American Democracy

Ninth Grade

Unit VIII. Forms of American Government and Outstanding Citizenship Problems
Unit IX. Waste and Conservation of America's Resources
Unit X. Immigration and Americanization
Unit XI. International Relations

Chronological and topical units.—In general, all unit plans are either chronological or topical. The unit plan developed on the chronological order takes the subject matter to be presented and divides it arbitrarily into ten or fifteen units. In American history, for example, the first unit would perhaps deal with the era of discovery and exploration from 1492 to 1607; the second unit might describe English colonization and would possibly extend from 1607 to, and including, the settlement of Georgia; and so on.

Even such a chronological arrangement, however, does not mean that the several history units have no relationship or connection. Units should not be considered solely in themselves. History is a merging process and must be so taught. Many of the causes of events in any particular unit may, and usually do, extend back into the preceding unit; the arbitrary lines separating individual units should be crossed readily to establish cause-and-result relationships. The development of history by the chronological unit method grows with time and develops horizontally from the earliest time to the present day. By horizontally is meant a broad swath of history in which a certain period is taken; and all events connected with it, be they social, economic, or political, are discussed in full before the succeeding period is begun.

The second method of the unit plan is the topical and is vertical in its approach to history. This plan takes a particular topic such as "Inventions" and, before another topic is started, deals with it alone either from the earliest time to the present or from modern times back to the earliest periods. It must be remembered, however, that the same danger exists in this plan as in chronological development. Many teachers will hold so closely to the topic or unit under discussion that it will become, in the mind of the student, a field of knowledge surrounded by insurpassable walls, an isolated field without contact with any other of the forces of human society. Events and movements in history are so closely allied that any artificial dividing line is indeed difficult to draw. It might be impossible, for example, to separate such topics as "Commerce" and "Industry."

No matter which method is used, the common sense of the teacher must at all times be prepared to change, to shift, to adapt subject matter to fit best the classroom situation, regardless of units that serve solely as a convenient tool in the teaching of history.

The San Fernando Plan joins the chronological and the topical methods into one by first completing the chronological study of history intensively and then using the

PLAN

Unit	1. Emphasis on historical movements	2. Emphasis on civics and government	3. Emphasis on social problems	4. Emphasis on cultural development
1 and 2	A perspective reading of an American history text during the first two months for review and orientation and for the identification of specific problems for the plan to be selected.			
3	The Westward Movement	The National Constitution and Government	Frontier Life	Colonial Art and Literature
4	The Struggle over Slavery	State Rights and State Government	Race Problems	The Concord School
5	The Industrial Revolution	The Growth of Cities and Local Government	The Evolution of Transportation	Science and Invention
6	Capital and Labor	Agriculture and Industry in Politics	Vocational Exploration	American Architecture
7	Imperialism	International Relations and Foreign Governments	Social Problems of Other Lands	Foreign Travel
8	The Progressive Movement of Roosevelt and Wilson	The Development of Political Parties	Immigration and Conservation	National Parks
9	America and the World War	The Rights and Duties of Citizenship	The Family and the Community	The History of American Music
10	Economic Rehabilitation	Government by Commission in State and Nation	Present-day Social Welfare Problems	Realism and Modern Poetry

topical units. In this plan, a chart of which is placed in this chapter, history is taught first chronologically as a foundation, and then the alternate topical plan is used. This plan gives a teacher a wide field of topics from which to select after the intensive study of the field is completed. No single plan need be followed unless the teacher desires it. If a teacher in any history department would rather teach civic, social, or cultural problems, he should feel free to do so. And, too, if at any time a topic is unsatisfactory to an individual teacher, he should be allowed to substitute another topic of his own selection.

The teacher should select one of the four plans from this chart for a year's work, giving approximately a school month to each unit. Or he may divide the class into four groups and give each group a different plan. The different plans should not be followed rigidly; students and teachers should feel free to change topics. It will be noted that all the plans are the same for the first two months in each semester. This is to build a foundation in history before beginning the topical work.

Other interpretations of the unit plan.—For the sake of simplifying the discussion of the method of unit organization, the unit has been defined and illustrated up to this point in its simpler and more obvious forms. More far-reaching implications that are insisted on by many progressive teachers will be developed in a later critical section of the chapter.

Before this seems feasible, it may serve the purpose of clearness if typical steps in instructional procedures that characterize teaching by the unit plan are explained.

METHODS IN UNIT-PLAN INSTRUCTION

Introducing the unit.—The teacher's first obligation in beginning a new unit of work is to arouse the pupil's interest by luring his curiosity or by getting him to recognize the practical values or vital uses the information to be studied may have for him. Two natural methods of introducing a unit, therefore, readily suggest themselves: (1) an inspirational, revealing, introductory talk or lecture by the teacher; or (2) a question-and-answer discussion with the class, showing the relation of the new unit to their previous experience or acquired knowledge or its vital relation to the pupil's present needs or to a present-day problem in which interest may be taken for granted.

The teacher of social studies should be able to give such an inspirational introduction or should at once begin the serious cultivation and practice of such a technique. The selection of some dramatic incident or of some vital crisis in the material of the new unit may be chosen to arouse the interest of the class. A teacher who cannot learn to do this cleverly and effectively in the social studies can expect little success in the teaching of any content subject. The human interest elements and the incidents of adventure and service are so richly present in all phases of the social studies field that any teacher should have little difficulty in making a selection that will arrest attention and give a recognition of vital values. Such inspirational introductions must not fall into the error of lengthy, explanatory lecturing. They should be brief ten- or fifteen-minute efforts, stirring, glowing with a spirit that shows the conviction of interest and evokes a contagion of enthusiasm.

The second device for introducing the new unit, the question-and-answer discussion, is intended to lead students to a recognition of real values in the content of the unit. The unit plan, aiming to cover systematically a broad field of subject matter, may, in this connection, be compared and contrasted with the so-called "activity plan," so commonly used in the elementary schools for motivating wide reading or study of content material.

In the unit plan the motivation must be somewhat more artificial than in that type of activity work where educative experiences are left to grow out of some real and vital present need of the pupil and where these needs compel somewhat random, accidental, and often unbalanced explorations into textbooks, reference books, or other available sources of information. In this respect the unit plan may be recognized as a compromise with the activity method, because the former still insists on the necessity of progressive, balanced study of one or several content subjects or of a more carefully organized field of information.

Since we cannot assume, then, that the study of a block of material is motivated by a spontaneous, natural demand of the pupils based on a present recognized need, the motivation must be supplied by the introductory discussion so that the recognition of values will be as clear and as hearty as a little thinking and discussion can make possible. This assumes, of course, that a well-organized course of units will have excluded most of the conventional topics for which such a ready justification is not easily made apparent.

In most of such introductory discussions whereby the practical reasonableness of the new content is to be demonstrated, some of the best unit-plan courses have utilized the values of the problem method, which is to be discussed more fully in Chapter III. Further, in the selection of the problems there has generally been a clever use of the compelling interest that may be expected if such problems have an obvious relation to present-day social, political, and economic needs and controversies. If such problem recognition is not obvious in the unit-plan organization in use, it should require little ingenuity to devise or borrow such a problem for the introductory discussion period for each of the units.

First reading for unit perspective.—The next step in developing the unit is to have all pupils do a piece of reading that will give them all a broad perspective of the field to be covered. Since, as a rule, the unit-plan courses in the social studies are grouped about some core subject, most commonly history, this type of organization will be the most practical as well as the most convenient to illustrate the importance of this step. The reading for perspective will be most easily made available in one or several textbooks in the core field. This first reading should have as its purpose the orientation of the student for other activities to follow.

The change from the common textbook recitation procedure to perspective reading for orientation and background purposes presents one of the most serious difficulties for both students and teachers. The fact that a textbook is used will tend to throw the students into the laborious, intensive study type of reading. It will be hard to induce them to use the more rapid, more superficial type of skimming helpful to the sensing of movements and outstanding important events and the disregard of massed detail which the typical textbook in the social studies usually attempts in its effort at cyclopedic completeness. Only a careful emphasis in the spirit of the teacher's assignment can obviate the alarm that students will feel over what will seem to be inordinately long study tasks. Frank explanations of the purpose of perspective reading, often covering several chapters in the typical textbook, and a rigid avoidance of unreasonable testing after the manner of the old recitation will reassure the pupils that unreasonable assignments are not involved. Several such experiences will be necessary before a class can be made to realize that the method of study has been radically changed. If a teacher cannot overcome the habit of recitation testing on such reading assignments, this step in the unit plan, and a most vital step, will be a failure. The unit plan will be wrecked in a deserved spirit of protest and rebellion on the part of most students in any class. The teacher must rigidly avoid detailed testing over such perspective reading, or the unit plan should not be undertaken.

Another device that will aid students in getting a realization of the value of this perspective preview is to give them a reasonable number of class periods to do this reading instead of assigning such work for home preparation. How much time to allow is a question of average estimates. Reading history material at the rate of 150 to 200 words per minute is a reasonable expectation for readers of average ability in junior high school grades and may serve as a rough basis of time allowances for senior high school classes as well. Even at the slower rate the average pupil should be urged to cover twenty to twenty-five pages in an hour's class period. From those who cannot achieve this it may be reasonable to demand the necessary extra time as a home-work assignment, in order that all the class may not be held back to the rate of the slowest.

Evaluating discussions.—When the rapid perspective reading, giving pupils a broad bird's-eye view of the scope of the unit, has been completed, it seems advisable to spend one or two periods in evaluative discussion. The caution against recitative questioning must be repeated in this connection. In no sense is this step intended to be in the nature of testing, and pupils must be kept from receiving that impression.

Much of the evaluating should be done by the teacher. Open textbooks in the hands of pupils will aid in facilitating the evaluations and will guard against students' getting a misconception of the purpose of the exercise. Point out the high lights; sweep through the movements;

suggest correlations in other subjects; become enthusiastic over preferences; betray special interests; suggest alluring possibilities for further individual activities in the unit. All this should serve a double purpose—to make clear and bold the perspective that students should have derived from their reading and to call attention to elements of interest that are to serve as the basis of the individual specialization to follow.

Planning individual work.—Out of the evaluating discussions pupils should come ready to pursue specific, individual study of topics of preferred interest. Volunteered suggestions and selections should be accepted and encouraged from all students if possible, although occasional negatives may be necessary for erratic whims. In addition individual conferences and, sometimes, arbitrary assignments at this stage of individual work may be unavoidable.

At this point the teacher will have to decide a problem of policy—How far shall this pursuit of individual specialization be allowed to range? Shall some or any pupils be allowed to develop a single engrossing interest? Or shall we require an intensified study of several topics and, avoiding duplications, insure that a well-balanced exploration of a comprehensive, predetermined list of topics will result for each unit in the course? Reasonable arguments may be advanced for either policy. Decisions will probably be made by the teacher on the basis of individual predilections growing out of past experiences and points of view. The subject-minded teacher is more likely to favor the latter procedure; the teacher under the spell of "progressive" theory will prefer the former plan and will argue that the true motive of unit-plan reorganization cannot be retained by the compromise that sacrifices pupil interest and initiatives to the demands of traditional, logical, adult organization guided by subject specialists.

Individual student activities.—Whatever method is followed in differentiating the individual stage of work under the unit plan, a variety of activities are available for the pupil. Some of these may be here listed. Some require no explanatory discussion; others will be taken up in connection with some of the general methods to be discussed in later chapters. By the time some of these relationships are seen in perspective, it will have become apparent that many of the newer teaching devices and pupil activities, as well as some of the best traditional practices, are adaptable to several of the general schemes described in separate chapters and may be used in various programs to attain the objectives of interest, civic preparation, and college requirements.

Such a list of student activities may include the following:

Free reading
Oral reports
Dramatization
Co-operative committee work
Problem solving
Discussion
Interviews
Field trips
Museums, places of historical interest, civic institutions
Construction of models and realia
Term papers or other written reports
Laboratory activities
Notebook and scrapbook preparation
Supervised study
Reports on related current events

Preparation for debates
Community activities
School government activities
Preparing exhibits
Attending motion pictures
Using workbooks
Radio listening
Map making and map study (desk and blackboard)
Making date charts
Large drawings for wall display
Picture portfolios
Large and small product and industry maps
Short, imaginary historical episodes, plays, and
   pageants
Drawing cartoons
Writing original historical short stories
Folk songs, phonograph and singing
Writing and delivering radio plays and talks
Historical puppet plays and pageants in costume
Letters and diaries in different historical settings
Real and imaginary newspaper articles of historical
   events

Class activities under the unit plan.—Much of the individual activity of students will have a double motive.
Chiefly the activity of each has been intended as a learning experience, a study, a gathering of impressions, a contact with information, a practice in skills, an acquisition
of attitudes or tastes, a discovery of new interests, or an
intensifying of old interests. But the activity may also
have an expression or sharing motive, an expectation that
the activity of each will culminate in some contribution
to the group. The ideal individual activity will generally
have this social outcome. If the individual work has been
driven to a desirable degree of achievement, the product

will be too rich for class audience, and the possible contributions of some may have to be neglected for lack of
time. The primary emphasis will always be on the values
of the learning experience rather than on the contributing
results. If either must be sacrificed, the latter will have to
be disregarded in some units; but all students must be
given their fair share of the opportunities to bring the results of their work before the class during the semester.
Conspicuous successes of the more capable pupils present
a natural temptation to favoritism in this as well as any
other plan of school work. There is the further difficulty
that interest in the reports and exhibits of others cannot
be expected to be as high as that which each student will
show in his own activity.

Summary of the unit.—The work in each unit should
be closed by some sort of summarizing activity with the
whole group. New evaluations, restored perspective, preparation for transition to the next unit, and possibly some
testing of results are essential.

Class discussions having these purposes in mind will be
the most common form of summarization. The teacher
will repeat some of the introductory evaluations with a
new emphasis that can now take for granted a more intelligent apprehension and response. Pupil participation
in this revaluation may be expected and emphasized.

Progressive summarization, cumulative and vertical,
of special interests and through succeeding units will be
advisable as the work proceeds through the semester from
one unit to another. Special attention to continuous
movements, general topics, fields of interest, progressive
evolutions will all be in place in the summarizing periods.
As developments unfold from unit to unit, reviews of
such topics in history, in industries, in inventions, in
literature, art, music, in political problems and issues may

be taken as typical of such cumulative vertical summaries.

CRITICAL EVALUATIONS OF EXTREME UNIT PLANS

Correlations in the unit plan.—Two elements have been taken for granted as necessary in a successful unit-plan organization of subject matter. One of these is the organization of all materials about a core subject. The other is the persistent correlation of all materials in any field of study with the central division of units. The second of these, however, is more essential than the first.

Thus far the discussion of the unit plan has been expressed in terms of subject matter, a point of view that may have provoked the antagonism of the more radical innovators, who insist that this involves a stultifying compromise with the fundamental spirit of true "unit-plan" reformations. The compromise must be here admitted; the question of a more thoroughgoing revision of teaching practice on "units of interest" is reserved for later discussion in this chapter. The compromising point of view has been taken for purposes of inducing favorable consideration for the more "progressive" plan, for conveniences of explanation, and for the sake of utilizing the concrete materials in the available courses of study that have generally recognized the difficulties of pedagogical pioneering and the adjustments necessary to get a degree of sympathetic co-operation from the more conservative.

To return to our claim that a generous use of correlation of various subjects is more essential than the selection of a core subject for the organization of a unit-plan course of study: In the social studies the fields of possible correlations are rather obvious, and the values in avoiding repetition and overlapping in teaching history, civics, geography, sociology, economics as separate subjects are equally obvious. The values of correlation, even if we keep the subject-minded point of view, can be indicated most strikingly if we take the simplest illustration possible. Let us assume that we have in mind such a simple unit-plan program as the combination of typical materials in the subjects of United States history and civics. What might be gained by such correlation? A comparison of the values of the two subjects from the point of view of practical ideas for training in intelligent present-day citizenship would probably favor the subject of civics. A comparison of the two on the basis of the objective of instilling permanent interests, or on the basis of appeal to natural interest, would certainly favor history with its elements of the human and the adventurous. The one would have the advantage of stirring narrative, the other the handicap of rather dull technical descriptions and explanations.

In projecting a unit plan for the correlation of materials in these two subject fields, American history and civics, it must be evident from the discussion of the plan in the earlier part of this chapter that either subject might arbitrarily be used as the core for a unit plan. Let us assume that for a particular school it has been decided that the good-citizenship motive shall be predominant, that all materials dealing with the structure and the functions of government, national, state, and local, and all civic duties shall be given preference in selection and emphasis. It might still seem desirable to use the historical outline as the organizing core for the unit plan. The choice of history as the core of the course does not necessarily imply or involve giving that subject the major share of time and attention. In fact, the relation of the two subjects, core and correlative, might just as readily and as feasibly be transposed, if one arbitrarily chose to do so for any reason. One might figure out similar reciprocal relations in an arbitrary correlation between materials usually included in American history and American literature, in the history and geography of our country, or in even more extensive correlations of several subjects. It seems more natural, however, to expect that the major importance will be attached to the core subject.

Degrees of correlation.—The general principle of correlation was first introduced into the theory and practice of American education by those leaders of pedagogical method a generation ago whom we now commonly refer to as the Herbartians—men like De Garmo and the Mc-Murrys who had been trained in German universities. As first introduced, the idea of correlation was applied to the bringing together in any lesson in any subject the materials that had previously been learned. The term soon began to be used in the distinctive sense of using materials in one subject to increase interest or understanding in another; it involved an inter-subject relationship, usually of pertinent known facts or related topics. With the growth of subject-mindedness and the specialization of training and interests of teachers in the highly departmentalized organization of secondary education, the principle of correlation has been given stronger support by theorists who consider it a desirable means of counteracting the departmentalized learning experiences of the child; but this advocacy has been met with an equally strong indifference by the specialized, subject-expert devotees. Ambitious programs of advisable correlations, especially between such related subjects as are included in the social science group, have been urged with enthusiasm by curriculum theorists and have usually been received with contempt and suspicion by specialized teachers. The common excuse for this rejection was the lack of time in allotted class periods to do full justice to the riches of one's own subject. The history teacher could not find time to teach civics, much less English features

like spelling or composition. The foreign language teacher
even complained when necessity compelled her to take
time to teach English grammar.

In the social studies even, teachers often refused to
recognize the interest and the clarifying values history,
geography, civics, literature, economics, the sciences, and
the arts might mutually transfer to one another, or the
chances that were often given to increase a student's
learning efficiency by giving him a chance to use or apply
in one subject what he had previously learned in another.
Such applications and interrelations were too often left
for the pupil to discover and work out for himself. In
fact, it has been more common for the extreme subject-
minded teacher to permit pupils to ignore or violate practices which were supposed to fall technically in the prov-
ince of some other department.

Many of the new plans of work in the social studies,
notably the unit plan and, as we shall see later, the problem method and the integration schemes are basically
intended to be comprehensive and detailed programs of
inter-subject correlations, either deliberately outlined by
expert prevision or expected to be achieved by the
exigencies of pupil needs and interests.

Broader scope of the unit plan based on pupil interests.
—Many of the unit-plan courses of study, however, have
attempted to free themselves quite wholly from any limitations set by conventional subject lines as traditionally
stereotyped by the logic of subject specialists. It seems
quite reasonable to predict from present trends in theory
and practice, especially in those schools which hold the
confidence of educational leaders as the conspicuous experimental centers, that within a very short time it will
be common in the public junior and senior high schools
to devote one-half of the school day to work now generally described as "social studies." The present experi-

mental organizations that have advanced to this degree of
emphasis have not hesitated to confine pupils to materials
commonly grouped in the subjects that are generally
thought of as falling in the social studies category. There
has been no limitation in the free, natural inclusion of
subject matter or activities usually thought of as belong-
ing to literature, science, sociology, economics, art, music,
physical education, or construction courses.

Such practices, and the educational philosophy that is
advanced to explain or defend this freedom in the correlation of materials, make it necessary, therefore, to re-
examine our tentative compromise in the description of
the unit plan from the subject-matter point of view. The
disregard of the subject divisions compels us to consider
what the progressives advocate about such practices.

In a word, this may briefly be summarized by saying
that the new theory is child-centered instead of subject-
centered. From this point of view we shall have to attempt a revision of our use of the term "unit." To such
advocates of extreme freedom in the revision of school
work the unit becomes a unit of interest or experience and
involves the study and use of materials without regard
to any consideration as to the school subjects under which
such information may previously have been classified.
Such a conception of education does away with the necessity or propriety of discussing units in terms of either core
subjects or correlated materials.

The explanation is now shifted to units in terms of
child needs or pupil interests. In doing this, advocates of
this type of unit-plan work have to meet objections as to
the sources of unit interests or the occasions of pupil
needs that will appeal as practicable to those who cannot
divest themselves of subject-minded predilections or
prejudices. The difficulty of meeting such objections has
given rise to the pedagogical controversies that have

raged about unit plans, no less than certain analogous theories involved in the project or the problem methods, or in the activity program, or the schemes for integration, all of which will in turn come up for more or less extended discussion in subsequent chapters of this book.

Fundamentally, all such controversies resolve themselves into a disagreement as to the point of departure. Shall the initiative or the motivation lie in the present interests and expressed needs of the child or in some imposed or inducted selection and distribution of interests fitting into a preconceived program of the teacher or curriculum maker in terms of subject matter? The most serious difficulty that advocates of the extreme, free, child-centered selection have to meet is the transfer of ideal programs to difficult public school conditions with large numbers and limited equipments as compared with the facilities of the experimental schools. Many teachers who are convinced that such individualized child-centered work is the true ideal cannot translate this ideal into actual practice without more or less serious compromises.

BIBLIOGRAPHY

Morrison, H. C.: *Practice of Teaching in the Secondary School.* Chicago: University of Chicago Press, 1926, Chapters X-XII, XVII-XIX.

National Society for the Study of Education: "The Social Studies in the Elementary and Secondary School." *Twenty-second Yearbook, Part II.* Bloomington: Public School Publishing Company, 1923.

Rugg, Harold O.: A series of six textbooks for an integrated unit course in the Social Studies for Junior High Schools, under the titles *An Introduction to American Civilization* (1929); *Changing Civilizations in the Modern World* (1930); *A History of American Civilization: Economic and Social* (1930); *A History of American Government and Culture* (1931); *An Introduction to Problems of American Culture* (1932); *Changing Government and Changing Cultures* (1932). Boston: Ginn & Company.

Swindler, R. E.: *Social Studies Instruction in the Secondary Schools*. New York: Prentice-Hall, Inc., 1933.

Wilson, Howard E.: *The Fusion of Social Studies in Junior High Schools*. Cambridge: Harvard University Press, 1933. One of the best recent studies of the unit plan; including a survey analysis of practices in a number of leading school systems, a review of the theory and history of fusion in the social studies, and a critical evaluation of the plan.

PERIODICALS

Gambrill, J. M.: "Experimental Curriculum-Making in Social Studies." *Historical Outlook*, December, 1923, pp. 384-406.

Smith, Gale: "Teaching History by the Laboratory Method." *Historical Outlook*, January, 1932, pp. 21-24.

PAMPHLETS

Rugg, Harold O.: *The Social Science Pamphlets*. Published by the author at Lincoln School, Teachers College, Columbia University, Second Edition, 1923-1926.

CHAPTER II

WORKBOOKS AND STUDY GUIDES

Evolution of the workbook method.—Workbooks may be said to be a by-product of several distinct movements in recent educational practice, notably the standardized objective testing and the supervised study method.

When the first primitive, objective, achievement tests in elementary school subjects were published (about 1910), the supervised study method had swung into considerable prominence both as an administrative device to meet the serious problem of retardation that research had exposed and as a classroom method for improving instruction. The supervised study movement was conscious, from the beginning, of the ideal of individualizing instruction as far as limitations of mass education would permit. Its chief aim was to give the laggard a chance to catch up without being penalized as heavily as he had been by repeating much of the work he had completed satisfactorily. Likewise, supervised study consciously aimed to free the superior child from the discouraging incubus of the laggard, by giving exceptional intelligence the chances for acceleration or an enriched program of studies while the slower pupils were struggling with minimal essentials.

Teachers dealing with diversified levels of ability in a typical class and attempting to achieve a general activity of study instead of the inefficient recitation soon recognized the value of concrete, specific assignments that would permit individualized progress in work without interfering with the study activities of other pupils in the room. The evolution, from the early efforts to give the assignment instructions to each pupil orally, to specific instructions on the blackboard, and then in the form of mimeographed work sheets, was a natural one as this assignment technique became more and more efficient. Ultimately this type of study guidance saw its perfected development in self-instructing textbooks, or in the elaborated printed work-plans or job-sheets of the Winnetka or Dalton plans, making the pupil practically independent in his study for a month's or a semester's work in a particular subject.

As standardized testing developed, parallel with this movement in supervised study and individualized instruction, it was soon apparent to those who were planning self-directing assignments and work-plans that many of the distinctive devices being used in the intelligence and achievement tests were highly practicable for the purposes of study guidance. These devices had certain advantages of objectivity and efficiency which were most economical in time for both pupil and teacher. In his independent work the pupil could be saved a great deal of trouble in recording reactions and solutions. His energies were not required for laborious copying or elaborate written solutions. Likewise, the teacher was saved much time in checking and grading the results of pupils' daily work without being required to spend weary hours in reading papers. Moreover, these devices removed much of the testing and grading from the unfair and inaccurate subjective evaluation that had been common in the oral recitation or the written essay type of work. In all school exercises where written expression was not an important consideration these standardized testing devices thus offered a chance for both pupil and teacher to achieve much more work in the regular class period.

Other important elements that came into the perfected workbooks, as these began to come into the market, were the more expert evaluation of subject matter and the progressive, balanced distribution of this subject matter in the assignments for a semester. Lesson-planning was directed towards achieving the standards that were being evolved, in a highly scientific way, by the makers of the standardized achievement tests. The makers of tests were not content with their own subjective evaluations of the important items in any subject, nor were these tests long based on principles of random sampling of abilities. Before standardizing a test, or while a test was in the process of standardization, the relative importance of items, processes, or skills was established by elaborate research into frequency of use or pupil difficulties, or by surveys of expert opinion.

When the earliest standardized tests and scales came into general use and were first used by superintendents and principals to survey the achievement of pupils in the schools, many teachers were first alarmed and then resentful at the tests. They realized that an efficient instrument had been invented to judge the results of their teaching. The efficiency of the new testing devices was recognized in spite of the fact that they sometimes wrought injustices in these school surveys because teachers could not always be blamed for results, the lack of ability or previous preparation often being factors as important as the effectiveness of the teacher.

The more enterprising teachers, however, instead of being content to treat the tests with suspicion and opposition, began to consider the advisability of using the tests themselves to prepare children for the ordeals of an administrative survey. In this practice the values of the test devices as efficient means of checking on the work of pupils and the evaluation of significant objectives were readily discovered. From the use of tests for coaching pupils in preparation for surveys, the steps to duplication, imitation, and adaptation of the tests for daily drills and for regular daily or weekly lesson testing were natural ones.

Thus the technique of the workbook and of the study guide tests was evolved in the classroom long before the device was commercialized and brought into common use. It was perfected to such degrees of simplicity, economy, and thoroughness that workbooks and study guide tests are now available and feasible for use even by teachers who have had no contact or experience with either supervised study or standardized tests.

The variety of workbooks available.—Workbooks and study guides are now available in practically every subject in the elementary and junior high school grades, in most of the high school subjects, and even in several of the more important college studies. In many of these subjects a wide selection of workbooks is on the market. Most of the leading school-book publishers have competing workbooks in all the elementary fields. In many cases specific workbooks are published for use with a particular textbook, and many of the newer textbooks incorporate testing or study guide devices for each chapter.

Workbooks have subject point of view.—From the preceding explanations it will be apparent that the workbook has, up to the present, been largely a subject-minded enterprise. In this respect it must here be recognized that this newer method of work in the social studies is somewhat different in spirit from the other methods that are being discussed. Practically all of the other methods may be described in general as efforts to get away from the textbook and subject-minded point of view. With rare exceptions, the workbook has not yet taken that direction. It is distinctive among the newer methods in having a rather conservative tendency as far as the revolt against logical subject barriers is concerned, or as far as freedom in the selection of content is involved.

This building of work and study guidance on subject lines is not a necessary characteristic inherent in the workbook, however. In fact, one of the newer series of textbooks in the social studies, which is very broad in its correlations and very free in its disregard of subject lines, is accompanied by a series of workbooks that are urged as a highly essential part of the course proposed. In curriculum revisions in a school system where it is considered advisable to lead a number of teachers out of a subject-minded attitude to an experimental approach toward the progressive, child-centered procedure, one of the most feasible means of revision may lie in the construction of study guides that will make the transition easier for those teachers who have not acquired the newer philosophy and who may have difficulty in laying aside their subject-minded bias or their habit of reliance on textbook materials in their instruction. In fact, many of the newer courses of study produced under the direction of progressive curriculum experts or teacher committees make a close approach to the workbook or study guide type of manual. These courses of study may be described as being elaborate semester lesson plans, prefaced by a modernized philosophy of objectives and including a readjustment of materials that not only tends to get away from a specific textbook or subject basis, but is usually replete with suggestions for devices and methods that fall just short of being such a workbook as might be put into the hands of pupils. In fact, the only clear distinction that can be made between some of these progressive curriculum revision manuals and the typical workbook is that the former is intended for use by the teacher, while the latter is intended to be used by the pupils themselves. With the development of the next step in the evolution of workbooks, the makers will then incorporate this third significant movement in recent education, curriculum revision, as well as the standardized testing and supervised study movements.

Indeed, in the social studies some of the workbooks have already achieved this stage of development. One of this type has already been referred to, and similar study guide materials, outlined on the unit plan and embodying various types of correlation of the subjects of American history, geography, and civics, with occasional supplementary excursions into other subjects, are in use in some school systems and are certain to be available for general use very soon.

Varying purposes in workbooks.—The workbooks in different subjects vary considerably in their materials because a variety of purposes may be recognized in them. Even in workbooks in the same subject there are sometimes widely varying materials because they are intended to achieve very different results. To illustrate this most strikingly and to demonstrate the possibilities for the future development of the workbook method in the social studies it will be necessary to describe some of the purposes and devices used in workbooks in other subjects as well as in the social studies field.

Workbooks for supplementary drill.—While drill work has been most prominent in the development of the workbook movement, it has, perhaps, the least value of all the possible purposes for the social studies. The function is most clearly seen and most frequently used in the workbooks in elementary school reading and arithmetic. Their use in these subjects must be briefly discussed not only to show their possibilities and limitations as a method in the social studies but as a warning against the use of workbooks in the social studies in the same spirit that might be desirable in these other fields.

In primary reading classes the workbook has become a desirable, efficient learning and study device in place of the wasteful type of busywork once used to keep pupils from idle disturbances while the teacher's attention was given to a small group for instruction. The workbook has solved the problem of seatwork in such a way that pupils not in the teacher's immediate instructional group can go on with reading experiences that will give original, independent learning contacts in effective supplementary practice in such a way that it is possible for the teacher to make a quick check on their activities and progress.

In arithmetic most of the workbooks supply a mass of supplementary drill problems. This makes possible a wealth of practice in the various processes to be mastered without having the pupil waste the bulk of his study time in copying examples from a textbook or the blackboard. The seatwork, done on the printed sheets of the workbook, is free from the confused, slovenly arrangement so often found in the child's arithmetic papers and greatly increases the teacher's efficiency in checking the work for errors and in grading the pupils' work.

Unless one has a very conservative estimate of the value of drill in the memorizing of facts, dates, and events in history, or similar data in geography or civics, it must be apparent that this method will have only a limited application in the social studies. It is true that some of the workbooks in the social studies subjects still show this tendency to emphasize the memorization of facts, but it must be admitted that to this extent the workbook is serving only to maintain a reactionary concept of the objectives in the social studies. If a workbook is used that makes such memorization and drill functions possible, the teacher will do well to give a careful consideration to the progressive educator's condemnation of such aims and practices.

Workbooks for self-testing and diagnosis.—Closely allied to the drill type of workbook is the material that is intended to make it possible for the pupil to test himself on what he has studied and to discover, and usually correct or perfect himself in, those elements which he has not understood or mastered.

This type of workbook material is again most conveniently illustrated in concrete form by some of the more carefully constructed workbooks in arithmetic. Diagnostic test pages, covering progressively expanding types of work in the different processes, are introduced at the end of weekly or monthly sections in such a way that each pupil can readily discover those difficulties or weaknesses in which he needs some further review or drill.

If we eliminate the drill motive in the social studies and assume a workbook that makes an intelligent evaluation in its test exercises of the most important elements, the workbook exercise on a particular chapter or period in history or in civics, or on a general topic or country in geography, may serve both as a helpful device for a pupil's independent testing of his reading or study and as an intelligent guide to direct him to an effective and economical rereading or review of sections in which the test shows his understanding or recall is imperfect.

Workbooks as a basis for remedial instruction.—One of the most serious criticisms that may be brought against our educational procedure in recent years is the failure of supervisors and teachers to apply the results of standardized achievement tests to the improvement of instruction. The vast possibilities of these tests for the diagnosis of pupil needs and for the application of remedial instruction after the giving of tests have too often been ignored. Standardized testing was started for administrative survey purposes. Even when it was demonstrated, by the development of diagnostic tests, that a much more valuable educative purpose might be served, many schools and teachers were content to let the testing end with this superficial result. It may fairly be charged that testing programs generally and most of the standardized measurement have been content with the accumulation of masses of interesting information in the form of impressive statistical tables and the medians, deviations, and correlations that were obtained by the statistical juggling of such tabular data.

Too commonly it has been ignored that the interpretation of such tests in terms of individual needs and the planning of remedial instruction on the basis of such individual diagnosis were, by far, the most important steps in a testing program. This was the last step, and certainly the most difficult, and was, therefore, often omitted, even when its importance was recognized. Because of this failure, the standardized tests, and even the informal objective tests, have never attained their true educational significance. It may be said that a single standardized test, if patiently diagnosed and conscientiously applied in terms of remedial instruction, could give a teacher results that would keep the most ambitious busy for a whole semester with any class. It must also be recognized that a single test, followed by such a diagnostic and remedial program, is of much greater value than a score of tests that never get beyond the stage of statistical tabulation.

One of the significant possibilities of the workbook has found expression in the realization of such diagnostic and remedial applications. Notably in many of the arithmetic workbooks we find the interest transferred from scores and norms to diagnosis and self-directing practice.

Similar values, with some conscientious study and direction on the part of the teacher, can be realized from the typical workbook in the social studies. If the study lessons are not merely used as convenient testing devices for grading the pupils on their daily work, the careful examination and summary of failures and omissions on various specific items in the workbook will reveal profitable suggestions for reviews, for improved emphasis in instruction, or for special supplementary or clarifying explanations by the teacher.

Workbooks for the teacher's testing of pupils.—Many of the published workbooks, perhaps too many, are constructed as convenient testing devices. With the convenience and efficiency that is made feasible by the use of the variety of objective methods of scoring, such testing manuals are used by teachers as a mere substitute for the labor of making their own tests and examinations and to reduce greatly the drudgery and uncertainty of marking and grading tests. This feature may be especially prominent in the workbooks used in the social studies. Some of this testing type in history and geography, especially those that are published to accompany a particular textbook, are devised as ingenious, exhaustive examination blanks that go to almost cruel extremes in trying to trap the pupil in the tests on details. An ideal book of this testing sort should avoid the emphasis on detailed catch questions. It should rather have the spirit of evaluating important essentials, and the ingenuity of the test maker should be expended in encouraging thoughtful reactions and study effort on the more valuable materials and methods of study.

Workbooks as study guides.—In fact the best type of workbook in the social sciences, as well as in any other content subject, should frankly be a study guide as well as a testing device. Teachers should use any workbook in the social studies largely for purposes of study guidance. Pupils should be allowed to have their copy of the workbook test to lead them in their reading and they should be instructed in the thoughtful use of such study guide tests. The most helpful devices of this sort will take the pupil over the chapter or unit assignment several times, with various conscious devices to lead him through his lesson and with such varying approaches and emphasis as will promote the most effective sort of concentration and reflection. Various testing devices for these purposes are the enumeration test for pointing out main topics and outlines; completion and multiple choice tests, and many of the true-false questions to promote careful attention to important details or to compel thoughtful consideration of significant relationships; the sequence devices for a careful noting of cause-and-effect relations, as well as the development of movements, and the thoughtful orientation in chronology; and various forms of the association tests for the necessary emphasis on relationships, cause and effects again, and the prominence of leaders and their achievements. All of these illustrations have been drawn from the field of history, but the study guidance values of these objective testing devices could equally well be illustrated in other phases of the social studies field.

Workbooks of this type, constructed and used in this spirit, are the most convenient and favored forms for assignments given in the job-sheet or work-plan form of class organization. In this form the pupil can be made quite independent, as far as teacher supervision is concerned, and the workbook can be trusted to make necessary evaluations of content and to train the pupil in a variety of study methods.

Used in this study guidance way, the workbook can function either as a basis for supervised study under the traditional subject form of work or as an effective supplement to help pupils acquire a general survey of subject matter where the principal effort is being directed to some of the more progressive attitudes.

Introductory bird's-eye surveys or effective summary reviews can be greatly facilitated by the use of such workbooks for supplementary textbook study in connection with some of the other general plans described in these chapters, notably the unit of interest plan, the problem plan, the laboratory activities, and the integration of the social studies with materials from other subjects. One phase of the workbooks in the social studies that has great future possibilities is the development of exercises in laboratory work analogous to the directions for map- and chart-making now included in some of the history and geography workbooks. Exercises in application of study materials to problems of judgment are also likely to see more extended use in manuals intended to be used in connection with the more progressive courses.

Workbooks as guides to collateral reading.—Another element likely to be given considerable development in future workbooks in the social studies is the guidance in collateral reading already found in some of the more ambitious plans for correlation and integration or in the more usable plans of unit organization. This type of development both in reading guidance and in devices for efficient checking on collateral is more likely to be found in the workbooks for high school courses than in the junior high school.

Workbooks used with new methods.—The subject workbook plan is adaptable to effective use with nearly all of the other new plans for curriculum organization and teaching method. We have already explained how the subject workbook can be used as a supplementing compromise in connection with some of the progressive methods. Here we are interested in showing how the history, geography, or civics workbooks may be used as a model for effective outlines or teaching and study guides with any reorganized program. One of the reasonable criticisms that has been made of the problem, activity, unit, or integration programs is the lack of balance in the selection and study of materials by pupils, especially when the child-centered interest is allowed to have free sway in determining the reading selections. Much of the danger or disadvantage inherent in some of these plans can be corrected by teacher- or committee-made study guides for the variety of study projects that may most reasonably be anticipated when pupils are allowed to do a great deal of individual work.

In many cases the newer methods of organization and instruction can be saved from the vagaries and whims of pupils by the preparation of such study guide direction sheets. One of the dangers of a transition to child-centered work, either when voluntarily undertaken by enthusiasts or when unwillingly followed under the supervision of administrative direction, is the planlessness of the work. Teachers often assume that careful planning is unnecessary, inadvisable, or impossible in connection with the new methods of instruction. Experience with such planless experimentation will soon convince any teacher of the fallacy of such an assumption. Blind or unpremeditated ventures of this sort usually result in despairing or disgusted condemnation of the whole progressive movement. Such unfortunate results can be avoided by intelligent, systematic planning for pupil guidance and testing in the spirit and with the devices evolved in a typical subject workbook. Moreover cumulative construction of such a series of study sheets, including collateral reading references, self-administering tests, and exercises in evaluation, can result in a more convenient and effective participation in the educative experiences that should result from self-initiated pupil enterprises in the social studies field.

Workbooks not mere busywork.—One of the most serious difficulties connected with the use of workbooks is the possibility that they may be handed out to pupils in the spirit of busywork. When we consider that the first workbooks in primary reading and in arithmetic were devised as intelligent educative substitutes for the futile and aimless busywork, it seems strange that they may now be converted in the upper grades to the same type of futile activity. Teachers who once kept pupils drudging at interminable notebook outlines and mechanically and copiously copying from textbooks in order to answer obvious informational questions may be tempted to use a workbook for the same type of primitive schoolkeeping. Such teachers are even loath to substitute a workbook for the more traditional sort of busywork unless publishers are willing to furnish a key for the marking of the books. It is obvious that for teachers with such unprofessional conceptions of educative values even a new efficient device may be abused. If the workbook becomes an end in itself, instead of a means to clearly understood educational aims, the cost of supplying them might as well be saved.

Workbooks in rural schools.—One of the exceptional values of workbooks has been demonstrated by their wide use in the social studies in the upper grades of rural schools. Where the teacher's attention has to be divided over the whole range of eight grades, and where the children in the lower grades need a larger share of her personal direction, it has been found that the study guide or workbook is an efficient aid in directing the older pupils in independent study of the content subjects.

Workbooks for special classes and pupils.—The adaptability of the objective testing devices as a means of in-

structional direction was early recognized by the teachers
and supervisors of special classes, especially in adjustment rooms dealing with retarded pupils or in rooms for
exceptional or slow children where it was considered especially desirable for the regular school work to be adapted
to individual needs or abilities. Such devices, which made
individual testing and diagnosis and especially self-testing and self-diagnosis by the pupil possible, were found
exceedingly helpful in aiding each pupil to cover a required course of material at a faster or slower rate than
that of the average class. In many of the experimental
rooms designed for this adjustment to individual needs
and abilities, elaborate self-directing lesson sheets were
prepared by experts or by the supervisors or teachers
specially selected for this particular kind of instruction.
It may even be claimed that the germ of the workbook
and study guide idea was first given expression in preparing materials for such classes and pupils.

Now that printed books are available in a variety of
forms for almost every subject, the inference is easily
drawn that such workbooks are especially valuable for
the efficient direction of the individualized instruction
needed in dealing with special groups or in facilitating the
work of retarded, exceptional, or slow pupils. For the
first of these the more rapid progress over the minimal
essentials of a course makes it possible to recover time
lost as a result of sickness, frequent transfers, or irregular
effort. In the same way the efforts of superior pupils can
be concentrated on required essentials in such a way as
to save a great deal of their school time for more extensive reading and explorations into difficult problems that
are quite beyond the limitations of most. The workbook
materials also help the slow pupil in several special ways.
They make study tasks very specific and concrete. As a
record of their progress is available, it becomes possible to

let dull pupils go at a pace slow enough for them to have a progressive success without being compelled to repeat whole semesters of work because they cannot do all of their tasks at the comparatively rapid rate of the average. The stigma and discouragement of daily failures and non-promotion can be greatly reduced by this device.

Bibliography

Bailey, D. C.: *New Approach to American History.* (Students' Guide Sheets and Teacher's Manual.) Chicago: University of Chicago Press, 1928.

College of Education, Ohio State University: *List of Workbooks, Teachers' Manuals and Other Instructional Aids.* Published by the University, 1931.

Klapper, Paul: *The Teaching of History.* New York: D. Appleton-Century Company, 1926, Chapters XVI and XVII.

Michell, Elene: *Teaching Values in the New Type Tests in the Social Studies.* Yonkers-on-Hudson: World Book Company, 1930.

Parkhurst, Helen: *Education on the Dalton Plan.* New York: E. P. Dutton & Company, Inc., 1922.

Ruch, G. M.: *Objective or New Type Examination.* Chicago: Scott, Foresman & Company, 1929.

—— and others: *Objective Examination Methods in the Social Studies.* Chicago: Scott, Foresman & Company, 1926.

Stormzand, M. J.: *American History Teaching and Testing.* New York: The Macmillan Company, 1925.

Periodicals

Kelley, T. L.: "Objective Measurement of the Outcomes of the Social Studies." *Historical Outlook,* February, 1930, pp. 66-72.

Krey, A. C.: "What Does the New Type Examination Measure in History?" *Historical Outlook,* April, 1928, pp. 159-162.

Lundberg, G. D.: "A New Use for the Laboratory Manual." *Historical Outlook,* January, 1932, pp. 26-28.

Monroe, W. S.: "Written Examinations and Their Improvement." *Historical Outlook,* June, 1923, pp. 211-219, November, 1923, pp. 306-318.

Pressey, Luella C.: "Needs of College Students in History." *Historical Outlook,* May, 1930, pp. 218-223.

Swets, H. A.: "Experimenting with the Unit Plan of Organization." *Historical Outlook,* November, 1932, pp. 345-350.

Wesley, E. B.: "Workbooks in the Social Studies." *Historical Outlook,* April, 1931, pp. 151-153.

Wilson, H. E.: "Worksheets as Aids in Supervised Study." *Historical Outlook.* October, 1929, pp. 287-291.

CHAPTER III

PRESENT-DAY PROBLEMS AND CURRENT EVENTS

The Method Explained

Various forms of the problem method.—In many of the new courses of study in the social sciences the problem method is combined or identified with the unit plan of organization. In such a program the principal large units into which the course of study is organized are consolidated under a single, comprehensive problem question, and, in most cases, divisions and even subdivisions of the unit are introduced by properly subordinated problems or questions, which are natural, logical phases of the more comprehensive general problem. In such a plan there is merely a substitution of questions for topics—inclusive problem questions for the main divisions, subordinate questions for subdivisions. In some of these courses it is apparent that there has been introduced merely a novelty of form; the units really resolve themselves into the familiar chapters and sections of the typical textbook. They are only slightly disguised by being given interrogative captions.

Even this primitive form of curriculum revision may, however, have certain values from an educational standpoint, though the changes in the presentation of familiar subject matter are merely or largely formal. One of the first possible values of the problem method may be achieved by this simple rhetorical device. In explaining this advantage we may take our first step into a more complete understanding of the possibilities of the problem method in its more ambitious developments to be explained later.

44

A recasting of topics into question form may be done in such a way as to increase interest in the materials on the part of students and compel a reflective approach instead of the more traditional readiness to memorize. Only a little cleverness in wording the questions, a slight insight into the meaning of a true problem, is necessary to formulate the material so as to achieve this superior motivation and secure this different study approach.

The meaning of a problem.—As an academic exercise a "problem" may be defined as a question that involves thought to obtain its solution, or that involves the collecting of information and a thoughtful digesting of such data.

The problem question, therefore, is different from the informational or recall question that has been very much overworked in school, in no subject more sadly than in the social studies. These subjects are replete with facts, and the temptation to make the class period a test of fact-memorization is very strong. The memoriter type of study in the social sciences and the use of factual "what" questions by the teacher seem to constitute a sort of traditional habit. The type of study and the type of question are subtly provocative of one another. Teacher and pupil, both, are often disappointed if either violates this tradition of method.

The problem question may be described as the "thought-provoking" question. It has been so called to contrast it with the "information-seeking" question. But the problem question may also be, especially in the social studies, a "research-stimulating" question. In either case, however, the emphasis is on the reflection or reasoning that is involved for the student. The facts involved may be the same for either the informational or the problem question. The former, as has been implied, is usually a "what" question; the problem usually has regard to some "how" or "why," an emphasis which can provoke a much more wholesome study attitude.

It is this change of attitude in both teacher and pupil that may be brought about by the simple restatement of a topical outline in problem-question form in any of the social studies. The pupil is challenged to think and search and relate understood facts for a new purpose, instead of blindly learning them for a testing exercise. The teacher is led to put less emphasis on memoriter reproduction of facts. The recitation is abandoned for study and discussion enterprises.

Present-day problems.—In a few cities the recent National Survey of Secondary Education found courses listed in the senior high schools under such titles as "Current History," "Problems of Democracy," "Economic Problems," "Social Problems," or similar terms.[1] Such courses, and similar suggestions made in recent years in some of the educational periodical literature, lead us to identify three distinct types of problem courses or methods as found in some of the progressive curricula. The first of these, already described as a combination of the problem method with the unit plan, we may designate as a "subject problem" course.

The second is illustrated by the titles given above, an impersonal but rather comprehensive selection of present-day problems—civic, political, economic, social, or any desired combination of these. The problems to be studied are real-life community, state, or national problems, usually of a permanent rather than ephemeral importance, an understanding of which is considered a desirable part in the training of intelligent citizenship. These problems are therefore assumed to have a rather vital interest to high school youth, and are considered to have

---

[1] Kimmel, William G., *Instruction in the Social Studies.* Monograph 21, National Survey of Secondary Education, p. 18.

unusual educative values because a study and discussion of them will involve an understanding of historical, geographical, or economic facts and principles. Such a study of any selected group of present-day problems, therefore, becomes a likely method of motivating a considerable amount of thoughtful reading in the social studies fields.

It becomes evident at once that the study of problems from this point of view will have to disregard some of the rigid subject divisions in the school tradition. This feature gives this second type of problem course a more advanced degree of freedom in the selection of study materials.

However, the ultimate possibilities of the problem method are not yet realized in this type of problem course, for the problems involved are adult interests and concerns and are teacher-selected, as a rule, or they are determined by a curriculum committee or expert for a course to be kept fairly constant over a period of several years, involving a large degree of uniformity in a number of schools or classes. They are therefore rather static and adult, and only theoretically real to the student. As a matter of fact, such a problem course may not be of any more vital interest to the student than if the topics had been encountered in a traditional progress through a history, geography, civics, or economics textbook.

Students' personal social problems.—The most advanced form of problem-method teaching, the third type we have in mind, deals with the personal, individual and real problems of the student, the answers to which he desires and is willing to seek. Most of these problems will originate in his current reading or in the circumstances and events of his school and community contacts. We are assuming, of course, a student who has serious curiosities and real interests in the social environment and in the events that impinge upon his daily experience.

From this we derive the real child-centered problem method of instruction in the social studies. It may be assumed that the teacher will be alert to utilize spontaneous suggestions of interesting problems that may come from any student in a class; or it may, with equally sound educational philosophy, be assumed that the teacher may take the initiative in sounding and suggesting pupil interests in current social problems that lie available in the life of the community or in the news of the day.

It is for this advanced type of problem exploration and research, both in real life or in the social studies literature, that the use of current events is suggested as a convenient, natural, and compelling point of departure for a real development of the possibilities of the problem method as an effective form of motivation and interest.

Supplementary use of current events.—The use of current events as a point of departure for the study of materials in the various social science fields, or as a means of approach and motivation for the study of such problems as have important historical, geographical, or economic backgrounds, must be distinguished clearly from the rather formal use that has been made of current news. The term "current events" has become almost a stereotype and as such includes certain implications as to the purpose and method of their use that involve unfortunate limitations on their possible value for the teacher or student of the social sciences. We seldom ask a teacher whether he "uses" current events. He "has" current events in his course, meaning that selections or clippings are made from newspapers, magazines, or miniature school papers published for the purpose, and that these are read, or posted on a room bulletin board, or are reported in topical recitations, and that these activities are engaged in for the purpose of giving all members of the class the information thus gathered by each pupil reporting. Occasionally the motive for such reports may rise to a somewhat higher plane to arouse pupil interest in present-day happenings, especially those having outstanding civic or social importance; or to teach pupils an intelligent habit of selective newspaper reading; or to show how some of the events of the past, or the machinery of civil government, or certain social studies information have important values for the understanding of everyday occurrences; or for the guidance of citizens in present emergencies.

In urging a more extensive and more vital use of current events, as is done in the paragraphs following, it must not be understood that these present formal uses are condemned. The more advanced program may not be feasible in many schools. If not, the use of current events for even these limited purposes is still of considerable value. In this connection it is necessary to point out that there is a wide range of practices in the extent to which current events are used in social studies classes. Some schools report occasional use of this material, especially during certain outstanding events such as presidential elections, openings of Congress, the passage of a much-discussed bill, a Supreme Court decision, and state or local elections. Some devote regular weekly periods, or part of a class period, to reports and discussions. Others go to the extent of devoting brief periods almost every day to some current news. All of these may be said to deal with current events as a supplementary phase of a social studies program, and all are to be distinguished from the method which uses current affairs as a starting point for the basic organization of a course in present-day social and civic problems.

The possibilities of using present-day events as a basis for the problem method in social studies materials far exceed the traditional uses and aims. Scarcely a week goes by that the average high school student cannot find something of vital interest to himself and most of his classmates in the news of the day. School journals issued for current events purposes never lack for materials of this sort. The value of such reading for both the immediate and the ultimate objectives of the social studies teacher have been greatly underestimated. From the point of view of motivating immediate interests in social science lessons, or for the more remote objective of training for future intelligent citizenship, the study, the discussions, the explanations of present-day problems can be made vitally practical. The future citizen can be made to realize that history in the making is not mere novelty, not mere news to report to his classmates, but that it is the human action that has present significance to him and will become history only if it has importance in the lives of those who will follow; that these events are brought about by men; that, if they are desirable, other men can promote them, if not, that men can change them. He comes to realize that history in the making is citizenship in action, for better or for worse.

In some of the papers prepared for school reading of current news, and in some of the magazines, we have had certain teaching or study helps. Usually these have been of the informational testing type, with occasional incidental suggestions of evaluation. This technique should be extended into a frank recognition that the current event may be used as a mere point of departure for reviewing or applying previously learned history or geography or civics. The event can be interpreted as a symptom or suggestion of a difficulty which challenges solution and therefore demands the investigation of new materials. This gives us a hint as to how the reading of current news may become the basis of a real-life problem-solving course of study in the social sciences.

The use of current events illustrated.—This use of current events as a form of teaching social studies by the problem method may be illustrated in some detail in order to make it clear that we are not merely dealing with the common use of this material as the source of topical reports presented in a simple informational way. From the newspapers and magazines the class committee selects a news item, preferably one of considerable importance, and one, too, that presents a definite problem in modern social life. This problem may be either local, national, or international in scope. Once the news item is selected, the next step for the committee is to state the problem by turning the headline from the newspaper or magazine into a "how" or "why" question. Let us suppose the news item read "Utah Repeals Prohibition Amendment"; the problem at once suggested to the committee might be "Why Was Prohibition Repealed?"

The next thing for the committee in the process of planning a program for the class would be to go back into history and trace the prohibition movement from the present to the past. This might require the assistance of the teacher, or the committee might be able to develop it themselves with the help of a good history text and its index. When this has been done, the reports are assigned to different students while others are appointed to lead the discussion after each report. The program of the class committee for any given day, therefore, might look like the following:

TOPIC FOR FRIDAY'S RECITATION

The Repeal of Prohibition

General problem: Why Was the Prohibition Amendment Repealed? (Meaning of problem to be explained briefly by the chairman or the teacher.)

The following reports are to be given by individual students on the topics indicated below. Each of the reports is to be followed by class discussion.

Report 1. Today's Account in *The Times*

Report 2. Editorial in Today's *Journal*

Report 3. The Wickersham Committee (P. 560 in history text.)

Report 4. The Eighteenth Amendment (P. 440 in history text and p. 320 in civics text.)

Report 5. The W.C.T.U. and the Anti-Saloon League (Find material in library.)

Report 6. The World War as a Cause of the Eighteenth Amendment (History text p. 540.)

Report 7. Trends toward Prohibition between 1850 and 1900 (See index in history text.)

Summary of the reports and discussions.

Supplementary Report 8. Jack London's *John Barleycorn*.

The lesson for Monday: Write a theme in class on the topic, "Why Was Prohibition Repealed?"

In the preceding plan it can at once be seen that the committee of students wished to approach the problem from a social and historical viewpoint rather than from one with a political science or civics content.

Let us suppose, now, that a problem was selected from the daily newspaper from which the teacher or the committee wished to develop a governmental or civic theme. The lesson plan might resemble the following:

TOPIC FOR TUESDAY'S RECITATION

The Tariff Bill

General problem: How Does a Tariff Bill Become a Law? (Meaning of problem explained by chairman or teacher.)

Individual reports for class discussion:

Report 1. All References in the Constitution to the Passing of Appropriation Bills

Report 2. The Tariff Plank in the Last Democratic Platform (See *Readers' Guide.*)

Report 3. The Tariff Plank in the Last Republican Platform (See *Readers' Guide.*)

Report 4. How Does a Bill Become a Law? (Civics text.)

Report 5. The Passage of the Bill in the House (See current accounts in newspapers and *Congressional Record.*)

Report 6. The Senate Amendments (References the same as for Report 5.)

Report 7. The President's Special Message on the Bill (Daily newspapers or radio.)

Summary of reports and discussion

The lesson for Wednesday: Write a theme in class on the topic "How Does a Tariff Bill Become a Law?" or "How Does the New Tariff Differ from the Previous One?"

It is not necessary, however, to follow a definite field in the development of a class discussion. The historical background may be developed concomitantly with the civic side, and, too, literature may be brought into the recitation to emphasize and lend interest to the problem under discussion.

It will be noted that the day following the type of recitation mentioned above is given to written composition wherein the student may not only receive practice and instruction in written expression but also summarize the recitation of the day before and express his own thinking in a carefully prepared theme.

Let us suppose, now, that either the teacher or the

class-planning committee wanted to develop all three fields of history, civics, and American literature in one lesson plan. And let us also suppose that the local daily paper for April 23 carried a front page story about an important occurrence in a near-by Indian reservation. The lesson plan would then be somewhat as follows:

TOPIC FOR THURSDAY'S RECITATION

The American Indian Today

General problem: Why Do the Indians Live on Reservations?

Report 1. News Item "Senate Committee Visits Local Reservation" (*The Record,* April 23.)

Report 2. One student will report on his visit to the Reservation last month with the Social Problems Class.

Report 3. How the United States Government Controls Indian Affairs (Civics book, pp. 248-270.)
Discussion on first three reports by the class.

Report 4. The Westward Movement and the Indian (History text, chapter 7.)

Report 5. The Indians in Cooper's Novels

Report 6. Helen Hunt Jackson's *Ramona*
Discussion leader—the teacher.

Report 7. Government of the Iroquois
Summary of reports and discussions by the chairman.

The lesson for Friday: Write a theme in class on any phase of Indian life in which you are interested or use the problem for today's discussion, "Why Do the American Indians Live on Reservations?"

In the development of these class discussions it may be found that one day's class period is not long enough to cover the material of the planning committee. In this case it is an easy matter to extend the work over two or three days or, perhaps, a week. Whether this becomes necessary will depend to a large degree upon the interest of the class in the topic under consideration.

Sources of Present-Day Problems

Sources for the study of current problems.—Several very good sources are available for getting the information about present-day affairs. The following are perhaps the most advisable:

Local daily newspapers, especially of the metropolitan type

Weekly news periodicals published especially for school use

Weekly and monthly magazines containing national and international news

Books on recent history

The radio

Movie newsreels

Schools and community events (by personal contact)

Each of these mediums has advantages or objections that should be considered briefly.

The use of newspapers.—Two general types of newspapers are available, one or both of which are easily accessible to all high school students—the metropolitan daily, and the local daily or weekly. Most of the small town papers, even the dailies, have little value as a source of material for school use. The only exception to this general statement is the accounts that such a paper may give of significant local events, such as elections and civic problems. The dividing line or criterion of usefulness may be said to be whether the local paper has or has not a regular national news service such as the Associated Press, United Press, or International News Service. Without this element the local paper will be of little value for school use.

The daily from a near-by large city, which may be accessible to most students, has a corresponding objection. Too much of the news in metropolitan papers deals at length with the city's crime and scandal that has only an ephemeral interest and probably too often, in yellow journal excesses, a deleterious effect on the interests and character of youth. Because of its sensational nature, as provoked by journalistic competition, it may at least be charged that the average high school student will be wasting much of his reading time in going through such a paper and will acquire the greatly distorted journalistic perspective of what news is really important. This criticism may even be applied to much of the telegraphic news printed in a city daily. A large part of the news sent out by the national service bureaus is of the crime and scandal in various parts of the country. The fact that an item has a date line and that expenses of telegraph or cables were involved, instead of being the feverish product of a local reporter, does not give it any more value. The event dealt with should be taught as the only criterion of importance. High school students may thus incidentally be taught the art of scanning newspaper headlines hurriedly and wasting little time on anything that is not of personal importance or permanent interest.

An advanced stage of such judicious scanning may be taught in connection with day-to-day accounts that may have little value until summed up in a final action. For example, three-fourths or more of the story of the parliamentary vicissitudes of an important bill in Congress have no value, as a rule, and much of this juggling and log-rolling over details may only serve to confuse an understanding of the law as it is ultimately passed. In some stages the debates may have significance, but again the student should learn to judge the news by its intrinsic values or its relation to permanent outcomes.

One of the advantages of the reading of daily newspaper accounts, in comparison with some of the other sources to be discussed, is that it gives students practice in realities and the raw materials of history and civics.

Other features besides the regular news columns of the daily papers deserve some consideration, either from the point of view of training students in their use as organs of citizenship, or as sources of material for problems in the social studies. The newspaper is an organ of opinion as well as, if not more than, an organ of information. High school students should be led to see that those parts of the paper that are especially intended to express opinion, the editorials, cartoons, letters to the editor, personal columns, and many of the signed articles by syndicated writers, are fundamentally dealing with current problems, either by way of explanation, argument, or indirect propaganda. The merits of these features as sources for social and civic problems should be made clear through direction and experience. The relation of these departments of opinion to the news itself should be scrutinized now and then to teach students how policy or partisanship shows itself, not only in the open declarations of editorials, cartoons, and the dispatches of correspondents, but also how it often subtly colors or disguises facts in the editing and headlining of the news.

The values of other parts of a typical newspaper for information, entertainment, or reference—the feature stories, especially in the Sunday papers, the market page, the sport page, book reviews, theatre, music, and art criticisms—should all be recognized as possible sources of problems in social, civic, and economic life. In some of these features, notably the sporting news, the comic strips, and the illustrated pages or supplements, the natural interests of youth may clash with the more serious evaluations of the teacher. Yet even these interests should sometimes be indulged, even as a source of problems for class discussion, for these attractions are always a part of the human pageant and with a little tact can be made to yield their values as factors in social life. Time should rarely be given such elements as events in themselves.

In this spirit even some of the most sensational crime stories, which will generally be disregarded, may occasionally demand attention as evidence of the difficult problems of justice and the maintenance of law and order, or as a basis for problems in morals, which are often a source of intense interest to the adolescent. As such, this type of news may be used as a background for training in ethical character. The chapter in our history that must record the emergence of the bootlegger, the gangster, and the racketeer gives a keen edge to the problems of official graft and corruption and the obligations of good citizenship to combat and reform such conditions.

The news magazines.—A few weekly magazines, like *The Literary Digest* and *Time,* and some of the monthly magazines may serve somewhat the same general purpose as the city newspaper in giving summaries of news and as journalistic organs of opinion. Such magazines, in comparison with the dailies, have, for school purposes, some advantages and some disadvantages. Their chief advantage is the comparative absence of objectionable crime and scandal news. Another advantage of a weekly news summary as compared with the daily is the perspective that the former has, which makes possible a condensation or omission of ephemeral details in the development of many of the events that are of special importance for social studies purposes.

On the other hand, these magazines are largely restricted to national and world events. They cannot compete with the daily in dealing with the state and local news that is often as significant as any for social studies interests. In addition, much of the world and national news is a stale repetition of what students have already gleaned from the newspapers if these are read. The magazine style is also usually more heavily adult, which often offsets the advantage it has over the newspaper's diffuseness of detail.

The miniature school newspaper.—The weekly periodicals especially devoted to the publication of news for school use have the same advantages of perspective and condensed summarization that the adult magazines have. They have, in addition, an advantage in being able to select articles for the specific purposes of school interests and to use, in general, a simpler style than the adult magazines. However, because of the necessary cost limitations, the size of the school newspapers is seriously limited, and there is also the disadvantage of staleness for such students as have access to a good daily paper.

The radio and current events.—Another important source of information for the discussion of current events is the radio. Only a few of the more progressive schools can as yet boast that this very desirable piece of educational equipment is available for students during school hours. Because of their programs for music appreciation, we have to recognize the great service some of the advertising sponsors and the broadcasting networks have done public education in stimulating the installation of receiving sets in the schools. Where this equipment is available, the social studies teachers should take advantage of this powerful agency of information no less than the music departments are doing for appreciation. It may not seem unreasonable, when we have discussed the possibilities of the radio, to say that a receiver should be available at any time of the school day for any class in the social studies.

We should first compare the radio with the newspaper and other sources for current events in order to realize its possibilities and limitations. As a general source for news information the radio is at present seriously handicapped by certain conditions which are sooner or later bound to be greatly modified to the advantage of radio broadcasting and to a realization of its greater possibilities. At present the general news summary presented by many local stations is of very limited value, largely because of the natural competitive jealousy of the newspapers. The news publishers can hardly be blamed for their efforts to restrict the broadcasting of news. If and when this is highly perfected, the daily newspaper will lose much of its value; it will lose subscribers who can then get the news on the air with less effort and without any additional cost; and the newspapers will rapidly lose their value as advertising mediums—all of which will mean their ultimate extinction.

Radio broadcasters, however, have no other general source of news themselves than the newspapers, and for national and international events they cannot use this source, since this news has been gathered for the papers at great expense by the Associated Press and similar agencies and is a valuable property right that cannot be infringed by radio publication. As a result many of the local radio news summaries are promoted and controlled by the newspapers themselves and have usually been so conducted as to make radio news broadcasts of little value to the listener because he has already read the item in the latest edition of the paper or because he is given only such a brief bit of the news that he must go to the paper to get a satisfactory account. The journalistic control of news broadcasts has also resulted in giving most of the radio items the same sensational crime and scandal emphasis that is given in the newspaper's evaluation.

The national networks, however, are indirectly combating this domination of radio news by their enterprise in giving listeners-in detailed firsthand contact with many of the most significant events in the news of the day whenever these events can be anticipated far enough ahead to make the necessary broadcasting arrangements. Chiefly this has included spectacular events in which there is a great popular interest, the football and baseball contests that have national or large regional importance, political conventions and campaign speeches, and addresses on important political problems by outstanding leaders. This phase of broadcasting is expanding rapidly, and the increasing army of announcers will probably soon become a body of news correspondents who will furnish the networks with an independent news-gathering and disseminating machine that will make the "newspaper of the air" a reality and a serious rival of the printed journals.

At present, aside from the controlled summaries, such news as the radio brings, the firsthand broadcasting of events, has a great advantage over the newspaper accounts of such events. Take such an example as a presidential message to Congress or an important political meeting. The radio brings us the reality, in full and exact detail, as well as instantaneously. This reality not only adds glamor to the interest of such important events, but it frees the event from all possibility of biased editing and interpretation. We are not left to the mercy of headline writers and editorial summarizers to draw our conclusions as to what elements were emphasized. In this way we now get much of the important raw material of our political thinking direct and free from partisan coloring. If we draw the wrong conclusions from this raw material, we cannot blame another for the distortion. We need no longer subject all forms of subtle propaganda to corrective criticism. So powerful is this direct contact that the only thing we need fear is that the political control of the broadcasting itself may pass into the hands of a political party that happens to be in power and that will use it to an unfair advantage in favor of its own partisan program.

Directing radio listening.—Under present conditions, if the social studies teacher expects to use the radio as a source of current events, and especially if this is to constitute a basis for the discussion of civic, political, and economic problems, certain principles of technique should be formulated.

If the listening is done at school, the teacher can have a direct control of selection, or it may be socialized by having the selection made by a class radio committee. The selections of such a committee should be open to suggestions or criticism of the class.

Many of the most important events that should be listened to cannot be made available during school time. A careful anticipative scrutiny must be made of prospective programs, either by the teacher or by the radio committee, and all members of the class should be urged to listen in on such features as may reasonably be considered a part of the students' "home work" for either the social studies or the English elements of their course. Perhaps one of the most effective phases of educational guidance the school can exert will be the direction of students' interests and tastes towards selecting at home the better radio programs, instead of the tawdry and banal. This may prove one of the most important cultural services of the school, no less in the control of radio experiences than in the selection of the better movies or the better books.

Movie newsreels.—Occasional use may be made of the moving picture newsreels as a source of current events material or as the point of departure for discussions of present-day problems. But the use will be very occasional, since this source must be thought of as a possibility rather than a reliable reality as yet. The selections are naturally of the spectacular and accidental, as far as the events are concerned. The chief value lies in the reality given to important personalities in the news and in the motivation of interests in persons and events. In some instances, as during the World War period or in the economic rehabilitation program of the Roosevelt administration, we could have included in the current news category the publicity or propaganda programs that were presented by the government to arouse interest and support for administration policies. The problem of civic co-operation or critical resistance to emotional appeals for support may make this medium of the moving picture reels worth considering as current problem materials.

The greatest difficulty with this source of current news is that student contacts with any particular event will always be accidental. No plans can be made by the teacher to arrange for all the class to see a particular reel, and the showing of certain events can neither be programmed by the owner of the theatre nor be anticipated by teacher or students. For a class, the only contacts possible with this type of material must be left to the responsibility of a special newsreel committee.

School and community events.—Another source of current problems for vital discussion may be found in the personal direct experiences and contacts of students with community or school events that involve questions of civic or social conduct. Problems of this sort should be considered significant because they are very intimate and vital and may have educative values superior to events that are remote or that may be strongly academic in their content implications. The use of this source and the frank discussion of such problems are urged because their significance in school and community life will offer wholesome analogies to the broader interests of citizenship. Events in school that involve school government, whether by student organization or by the official administration, are of special importance in the practice of proper reasoning and in the development of desirable citizenship attitudes.

Other sources for present-day problems.—In addition to the sources that have been discussed, a more academic and more systematic course in present-day problems may be planned around sources not so directly related to current news elements for their point of departure and motivation. In many of the magazines which are not devoted to the summarizing of news, but which may be said to be devoted wholly, or in large part, to articles of opinion, usually by authorities or experts, we may recognize a source of supply for problems in all fields related to the social studies—economics, politics, international relations, or broader social questions than are involved in specific events. Along with magazines of the more serious adult type, such as *The Atlantic Monthly, Harper's Magazine, The Forum,* the *Review of Reviews, The Nation, The New Republic,* and others of this sort, we might include some of the books devoted to general discussions or surveys of recent or present-day problems.

Much of this material is too adult and too technical for general high school use. It will be much more suitable reading for the teacher as equipment for the kind of problem course we have been describing. Occasional articles, however, may be suitable for student reading. One of the best educative services a social studies teacher can perform, for at least the brighter students in senior high school, is to make them familiar with these magazines, which the cultured and public-spirited adult considers the sort of reading he can pride himself on in his social contacts.

In these magazines the teacher and some students may discover problems of special importance that would not become apparent even to the intelligent adult reader in his hurried contacts with newspapers and news magazines. The problems revealed and discussed in these more serious magazines of opinion are often the product of the profound reactions of experts to the events and movements of the day.

As an easy introduction of high school students to these ultimate sources of social reflection, it might be suggested that a social studies teacher could make good use of the *Reader's Digest,* the little magazine which gives us a chance for cursory browsing in a wide range of magazine literature by its monthly series of selections and condensations of many leading articles of the type that is suitable for a course in present-day problems.

A typical issue of the *Reader's Digest,* selected at random, may be taken to illustrate the possibilities of magazine literature as a basis for a present-day problems course. The *Reader's Digest* for November, 1933, in a list of thirty-two articles, included the following, with each of which we are suggesting related social studies problems:

"Our Pernicious Virtues," by I. A. R. Wylie, condensed from *Harper's Magazine,* suggests such problems as, What is wrong about patriotism? Is physical courage really a virtue? Is fidelity really a virtue? What are the relative values of charity and social justice?

"Streamline," by Daniel C. Sayre, condensed from the *American Mercury,* introduces the recent modifications in automobile construction, a problem in the field of rapid transportation.

"How To Make a Gangster," by William G. Shepherd, condensed from *Collier's.* The title itself suggests the problem.

"Turkey's Abraham Lincoln," by Stanley H. Howe, condensed from *The American Spectator*, a stirring account of great changes in Turkey since the World War, and a study in the problem of civic leadership.

"How Politicians Steal Elections," by Frank R. Kent, of the *Baltimore Sun*, a revelation of "the new art of election thievery, by which the political machine has fixed the result even before you vote."

Six or eight other articles in the same issue might just as well have been used to illustrate the possibilities of magazine materials easily available wherever there is a good public library.

SOME PRACTICAL SUGGESTIONS ABOUT METHOD

Some principles of selection.—In the sections immediately following it is proposed to give a number of practical suggestions about the selection, study, reports, and discussions of present-day problems drawn from the students' contacts with various forms of current literature, the sources discussed in the sections just preceding.

First we may take up some of the principles for the selection of materials. Fundamentally, of course, it is assumed that only such events will be selected, either by the teacher or the student program committee, as have some direct connection with the social studies course—items or articles dealing with economic, political, civic, historical, geographical, or broad social interests. The selection of events and problems should not be confined to the United States, even in an American history course. Foreign affairs, even when not directly involving our own international relations, are a part of the necessary present-day social-cultural interests of secondary school students. Even if our isolation in international relations may be justified in theory, that theory cannot be used to defend a provincial ignorance about important events in other countries. We might as reasonably expect a newspaper whose editorial columns ring with the slogan of "No entangling alliances" to banish all foreign news from its pages. The only circumstance under which a teacher would be justified in ignoring all but national news and national problems in such a course would be the existence of a definite world history course for which such materials were reserved for treatment. Even then duplication would be justified if events in any other country clearly had important bearings on our international relations.

In the selection of problems it is further advised that events of continuing and persistent value be given preference over those of temporary importance or ephemeral interest. On the other hand, too much time and attention should not be given a few events or problems. There should be a happy medium between variety and a thoroughness that leads to monotony, between a superficial hodgepodge of miscellaneous items and a restriction that will lead to narrow or specialized hobbies.

To prevent a limited selection with unbalanced emphasis on a few problems, on the one hand, and a miscellaneous, random scattering of interests, on the other, the teacher should have a tentative, elastic repertory of typical, desirable problems and should direct individual selections personally or by subtle suggestion to the class program committee.

Reading and study directions.—A few brief, practical suggestions may be worth while also with reference to the reading and study activities of the class:

In the reading of current events give special attention to national elections, acts of Congress, acts of the President, and Supreme Court decisions. See that students formulate the problems and issues involved in platforms, laws, vetoes, messages, and decisions and that the class or designated students trace the historical and civic background in textbooks or collateral reading.

Assign student reports or plan class discussions that will compare and contrast such national current events with related historical events dealing with the same problems or with the structural or functional constitutional topics involved.

Where a sufficient number of copies of a special paper dealing with current events is available for the whole class, specific articles may be assigned for hurried silent reading by all, and brief objective tests may be given on the reading. Such a test might include the formulation by the students of the problem involved and suggestions as to related history or civics topics that should be reviewed in the textbook or be assigned for collateral reading and report. In such a test an opportunity may be given for motivated practice in the art of using the index of one or several textbooks to locate specific related sections.

One part of the study exercise in connection with current events should be some correlated work in geography and English. Occasionally or regularly, as the teacher may consider advisable for any class, students should be required to locate on a map, and sometimes identify by brief informational description, the places referred to in their current events reading. Similarly pupils should be held responsible for an intelligent use of the dictionary for the pronunciation of proper names or other important terms. Lists for special spelling activities should also be a regular feature of the study activity of pupils. The use of the biographical and pronouncing gazeteer supplements of the dictionary should be made matters of effective practice and self-determined initiative as the students may be conscious of their individual needs along these lines. Exercises of this sort may be extended by requiring the use of important social studies terms in written or oral sentence construction. All of the exercises suggested in this paragraph can be related to current events materials heard on the radio as well as those read in newspapers or magazines.

Managing student reports.—Much of the work in current events should be brought into the class period by means of individual oral reports.

One desirable method of securing reports on current events is obtained through assigning a specific general topic, such as the tariff, financial problems, important events in specific foreign countries, and the like, to individual students to keep scrapbooks on and to report on from time to time. This is suggested merely as a possible alternative device.

In connection with some of the more important happenings, especially of national or international interest, the material may be used for open discussion in the class.

The responsibility for making reports on current events should be fairly distributed to all members of the class. The exercise in oral expression, motivated by a vital content, is one of the exceptional opportunities that should not be confined only to those who can already do this effectively. Some adaptations in assignments may be possible and may be justified to secure from some students the inspirational, interest-arousing results, and for others the opportunity for practice in expression.

Some systematic routine should be provided for the criticism of reports made to the class. The method recommended is the socialized one—a committee of critics composed of class members. Criticism of this sort should be trained to be impersonal in spirit. Corrections of mispronunciations, faults of posture, and grammatical errors should be made abstractly by merely calling attention to the facts and stating the correct form. The teacher must exercise great tact in this type of criticism to prevent the display of priggishness in the critics or resentment in those corrected. Such committee reports can best be made after the discussion on any topic has been closed. This criticism may be supplemented, as the teacher considers necessary, by individual information given to students by the teacher either in personal conference or in a brief written note. Misinterpretations or incorrect statements of facts in the report may be corrected by any student in the discussion following the report.

Conducting class discussion of problems.—The general class discussion following reports on current events may be conducted either by the teacher or by a student chairman. The latter, the socialized form of discussion, will be dealt with in the next chapter.

Basically the class discussion should proceed to deal with the problem involved in the report, not with the facts in the event itself. It will, therefore, be highly essential that the problem shall be identified by clear statement at the very outset. This may be done by the teacher, the reporter, the program committee, or by any member of the class.

As soon as the problem is recognized, the discussion should proceed by spontaneous, voluntary contributions from any member of the class. Comment by the teacher to interpret or guide the discussion will be in order at any stage. The only cautions that need be made are that the discussion should never be directed into a recitation exercise; that the teacher should try to avoid an indoctrinating attitude; and that the teacher should never dominate the thinking or discussion.

To prevent the discussion from becoming wearisome to the class the device may be adopted that any student has the privilege of demanding a class vote on a closure by raising both hands.

When the decision is made to close the discussion, either by the teacher, the student chairman, or a class vote, the results of the discussion should be briefly summarized. If the report, the problem, and the discussion have involved matters of special importance, this summary should be made by the teacher. At discretion, the closing summarization may be assigned to one of the students.

It should be kept in mind that the time devoted to a discussion of current events is justified not only because of the immediate information that it gives the students about these events and the occasion or background that it affords for the explanation and application of their studies in history and civics, but also because the cultivation of a permanent interest in, and a permanent habit of reading about, matters of civic and political importance should be taught as a part of the preparation for good citizenship.

CRITICAL EVALUATION OF THE PROBLEM METHOD

Importance of problem-solving in social studies.— There are decided practical reasons why problem-solving, whether it is based on the informal free method of current events, or whether it is based on a more formal selection of problems, should be given special consideration in the teaching of the social studies. We cannot hope during school days to provide students with a complete equipment of facts and solutions to prepare them adequately for efficient citizenship. Industrial, economic, and political conditions are changing so rapidly that we cannot foresee the nature of the most pressing problems that are certain to confront us even within a few years. The effective citizen is not the one who has learned what the problems of the past have been and how they were solved, but the one who has learned how to solve new problems, how to gather information, and how to arrive at independent solutions of new questions.

It seems highly necessary, therefore, that, in the preparation for efficient citizenship, the technique of problem-solving should be mastered by correct and effective practice in this intellectual art. It should also be evident that such practice can be secured more effectively by dealing with unsolved, vital current problems than by tracing the steps in a solution that has been worked out at an earlier day. The latter may have an important place for the inductive teaching of the problem-solving method, but the practice on present-day problems surely will have superior advantages in both interest and effectiveness.

This method also puts the teacher in a more scientific and open-minded attitude with reference to current political and economic issues that involve a strong partisan bias. The teacher of the social studies is often tempted to use his professional position to indoctrinate students in civic matters, or he is put under pressure by active minorities to promote such doctrines, either static or radical. The use of the problem method makes more possible an impartial, unbiased consideration of such questions and leaves the students free to form their own conclusions or develop their own convictions on controversial issues—a much fairer, more wholesome, and more educative procedure.

When the problem-solving method is used for the explicit purpose of training students in the method, they should be made definitely aware of what is being done and of the purpose that the practice is intended to promote. A more or less specific formal training in the discovery and clear formulation of issues, purposeful activities in collecting and evaluating evidence, the practice of open-minded deferring of final conclusions in some cases, and the consideration of resulting attitudes or actions, sometimes hypothetical, sometimes actual, should all be encouraged as conscious elements in effective practice. The values of the method for future use should also be made clear.

The problem method is selective.—One of the outstanding advantages in teaching the social studies by the problem method is the elastic, selective character that is given a course. Larger freedom is given the teacher in adapting time and emphasis to materials in order to suit the interests and needs of pupils or to give students a greater freedom of initiative and persistence in following special interests. Indirectly this freedom also involves a more desirable adjustment of materials to individual instruction or study.

One of the increasing difficulties in most of the social studies courses, especially in history and geography, is the embarrassing, almost confusing, wealth of material available. This excess of materials has resulted in making many of the textbooks in these subjects encyclopedic in their effort to crowd in details. Worshiping the fetish of completeness, as so many subject specialists are prone to do, or suffering from a fear of being judged unscholarly because of heroic omissions, the textbook writers in the social studies have too often destroyed any chance of a student's getting a reasonable perspective or an understanding of the relative importance of facts or events. Not even the cleverest use of typographical devices has been successful in enabling students to get a clear evaluation of sections and topics. Such courses have been described in the recent National Survey of Secondary Education as taking "pupils on a 'world tour' with fleeting glimpses of all past and present peoples and nations in their manifold activities and relationships." [2]

Unless a course of study built on the problem plan requires a teacher to take up all problems with all pupils, in the traditional stereotyped way—usually progressive curriculum-makers do not require this—the program opens up opportunities for selections and adjustments that are very difficult in the textbook-controlled courses.

Social and moral values of the problem method.—An even more comprehensive and lofty motive than mere civic efficiency may be advanced for urging the training of high school students in the art of problem-solving. The broader social efficiency and moral intelligence of students can be enhanced by a readiness and fluency in this important technique.

Many of the outstanding problems in the social studies have important ethical implications that are far more significant than the factual elements. Moral character is partly a matter of habits that have become automatic— they are no longer consciously controlled. This basic element is largely the result of the training and experience of childhood, as directed and controlled by the authority and example of parents, teachers, and associates of the elementary school period. On this substructure, however, is built that part of the ethical structure which controls conduct by social reasoning and intelligent choice. The design and construction of this superstructure of character is largely determined during the secondary school period. In this social and deliberative stage the content and methods of instruction in the social studies can play a more direct part than any other single academic factor. The social subjects deal with institutions and relationships that are much broader in their social importance

[2] Kimmel, William G., *Instruction in the Social Studies,* Monograph 21, National Survey of Secondary Education, p. 2.

than the questions of government or politics or citizenship. Questions of social justice, of the distribution of wealth, of the protection of health, of the prevention and punishment of crime, of racial and sectional tolerance, of public charity and philanthropy, of the protection of the underprivileged, of the prevention or reformation of delinquents—all lead into social fields that involve high moral judgment and attitudes.

For all connections that the individual may have with such moral issues, and for all decisions that he must make on them, a memory of the facts of history, geography, or economics is not nearly so important as a method of approach that will insure interest, open-mindedness, reflection, and independent decision. Students should have been trained how to use new facts to form new decisions for the new problems that will constitute the social and moral questions of their day.

BIBLIOGRAPHY

Counts, George S.: *Dare the School Build a New Social Order?* New York: The John Day Company, 1932.

Darrow, Ben H.: *Radio the Assistant Teacher.* Columbus: R. G. Adams, 1932.

Dewey, John: *How We Think.* Boston: D. C. Heath & Company, 1910.

Fancler, D. G., and Crawford, C. C.: *Teaching the Social Studies.* Los Angeles: C. C. Crawford, University of Southern California, 1933.

Institute for Education by Radio: *Yearbooks: Education on the Air.* Columbus: Ohio State University.

Kimball, R. S.: *Current-Events Instruction.* Boston: Houghton Mifflin Company, 1929.

Klapper, Paul: *The Teaching of History.* New York: D. Appleton-Century Company, 1926, Chapters IV-VIII.

Pierce, Bessie L.: *Citizens' Organizations and the Civic Training of Youth.* Part III of the Report of the American Historical Association Commission on the Social Studies. New York: Charles Scribner's Sons, 1933.

Tryon, R. M.: *The Teaching of History in Junior and Senior High Schools*. Boston: Ginn & Company, 1921, Chapter X.

Wood, Ben D., and Freeman, F. N.: *The Motion Picture in the Classroom*. Boston: Houghton Mifflin Company, 1929.

PERIODICALS

Lewis, J. J.: "Socializing the Newspaper." *Historical Outlook*, November, 1927, pp. 331-332.

Lewis, Virginia: "Building for World Citizenship Through the Social Studies." *The High School Teacher*, November, 1932, pp. 353-354.

Minor, Van Lieu: "An Experimental Course in Current Events and Problems." *School Review*, April, 1920, pp. 298-309.

Vannest, C. G.: "Experiments in the Use of Current Events." *Historical Outlook*, November, 1925, pp. 332-334.

Woodruff, Hazel M., and Crawford, C. C.: "Methods of Teaching Current Events in High School." *Historical Outlook*, December, 1928, pp. 385-390.

PAMPHLETS

Handbooks of Citizenship. McKinley Publishing Co., Philadelphia. Pamphlets on prohibition, farm relief, tariff, internationalism, political parties.

Public Policy Pamphlets. University of Chicago Press. Pamphlets on balancing the budget, technocracy, unemployment insurance, war debts and deflation, and the capital levy.

Unit Study Booklets. American Education Press, Columbus, Ohio, and New York City. Booklets on the depression, economic planning, unemployment insurance, crime, and services and cost of government.

CHAPTER IV

SOCIALIZED METHODS AND MANAGEMENT

Socializing purposes in teaching.—In this chapter it is proposed to discuss a number of devices and methods, both in class management and instruction, that are unified by a common specific purpose—the improvement of the students' social attitudes and the promotion of social practices. This motive is not modern; yet the progressive movements in recent years have all emphasized this objective and have exhibited great ingenuity and insight in inventing means to promote this aim by a variety of adaptations in class management and teaching methods.

These socializing factors are intended to enforce the ideas of civic responsibility that pupils may get from the content of school courses. We expect this content to be specially emphasized in the social studies materials. Similarly, it may reasonably be required in such courses that special arrangements shall be planned so that, as a result of social co-operation in the classroom, pupils will have had effective training in activities and attitudes that will help them learn how to live and work together in society.

Relation to the socialized recitation.—To a large degree the general method we are here dealing with may be said to be an extension of the socialized recitation that has been in vogue for a decade or more. We have in mind the same purpose as well as many of the same activities. Yet there is more involved. There is an extension or evolution of the socialized recitation, perhaps an adaptation of such methods to more advanced classes, perhaps an inclusion of practices that have been developed under the concept of student government as a form of administration or school management, perhaps an incorporation into the class program of real-life civic and social activities in the community as well as the school.

From this point of departure it may be said that in this chapter we have in mind three distinct elements of socializing methods and devices, of which the socialized recitation is really only one element, the second in this list of three. These phases are:

I. Socializing Class Organization and Management

II. Socializing the Pupils' Study and Recitation Experiences

III. Promoting Real-life Socializing Activities and Experiences

Each of these may be subjected to explanation, analysis, and illustration in the succeeding sections.

Socializing Class Management

A new conception of class management.—In putting the emphasis on the socializing purpose and in adopting a program that will promote this in all relationships of the students—to the teacher, to each other, to the school and community—the teacher will see himself function in a new spirit, as a guide, director, co-operator, rather than a taskmaster, a tester, and a guardian of discipline. Planning and suggesting for students to co-operate in execution will become the more characteristic part of class management. A social routine will take the place of a teacher-dictated routine. What specific tasks are to be undertaken by particular students will be arranged by the students themselves.

Sometimes this may be done by the representative plan, that is, by having activities planned and assigned by committees; sometimes by the dictatorship plan, in which a single student plans and executes; sometimes by a purely democratic arrangement, in which the class acts as a committee of the whole to discuss and decide problems of management.

As a general rule the first of these is the most feasible; the second and third will be used only occasionally for illustrative purposes. The objective is largely to teach by comparative experience the leading elements and values of the political forms prominent in government experiments in the world at the present time.

In the committee, or representative, model of class management, the students will co-operate largely through their representatives in various committee actions. By frequent changes in committee membership all students will have the experience of group leadership as well as social co-operation and the observation and criticism of representatives.

Students co-operate through committees.—The committee plan, then, is the most feasible fundamental arrangement for a socializing organization for class management. This plan will recognize both the official responsibility of the teacher and the motive of giving students social experience and training by the distribution of responsibilities for arranging and executing activities.

The plan may be provisionally explained by giving a list of possible committees, with a brief statement of the functions of each.

A planning or program committee.—An executive committee or board of directors may be chosen to take charge of class management and activities. Its functions include the selection of topics, current events, and problems that are to be studied and discussed; to make individual pupil assignments for special readings and reports; to relate such specific selections and assignments to the general field to be covered in a unit, month, or semester; to outline in advance daily lesson plans in detail; to select the chairman for each day's work and to acquaint him with the day's program; to direct and advise other committees; to instruct their successors; to give students references or sources for their assignments; to act as hosts to all visitors coming into the class; and to file a daily report of programs as planned and executed, for the teacher's records and for the next semester's committee.

The attendance committee.—The principal duties of this committee are to keep the daily attendance record and make the required report to the school office; to perform any recording of grades reported by the teacher or program committee; to send notes for the class to members absent on account of sickness; to attend to the make-up work required of absentees; and to instruct new students entering the class late as to methods and requirements.

The room committee.—The members of this group have charge of all conditions in the room and of all equipment except the classroom library; they attend to ventilation, temperature, lighting, and other factors of comfort; they are responsible for decorations, drapes, pictures, and any other artistic factors; they supervise and have authority over orderliness and neatness of students' desks; they see that blackboards are kept clean and have charge of all wall maps; they regulate any changes in seating of pupils made necessary by defects of eyesight or hearing.

The library committee.—This group has the care of all books in the room library; arranges for the loans of books from the school and public libraries; plans the special library lessons with the teacher and librarian; arranges for all class periods in the school library if special arrangements are necessary; works out special problems for research; and has the responsibility for developing interest in "browsing" and free reading.

The visual education committee.—This committee looks after the room bulletin boards and picture portfolios and all facilities available for the use of visual materials, stereopticon lanterns and slides, and moving picture machines and reels. Members of this committee should, if necessary, qualify by training and license to operate projection machines. They should arrange for the selection, procuring, and return of slides and reels available in the city visual education department or state university loan division. They should take charge of the preparation of maps, charts, and pictures as stereopticon slides if a lantern is in use. This committee should also have responsibility for making or securing reports on movie newsreels of interest and importance, and should keep the class posted on any good general films. The general spirit of this phase of the committee's work should be to encourage wise selection and good taste in attendance at the theatres.

The radio committee.—This group will have charge of all radio programs if there is a receiver in the room. Its members should consult some of the weekly and monthly radio periodicals for all broadcasting features that may have value or interest for a social studies class, and should check on the radio news column in the metropolitan daily papers for any local or regional programs that may be important. They should have regular opportunities to report such programs or features to the class and to advise what should be listened to outside of school hours, in some cases assigning responsibilities for reports on important addresses or events. There should be cooperation between the radio and program committees of the class for general preparatory or follow-up programs on important radio events.

The testing committee.—The duties of this committee will vary considerably as the judgment of the teacher may determine, depending on the grade and ability level of the class. The duties are better suited to pupils of exceptional ability in the senior high school; in junior high school a committee of this nature is hardly feasible. It seems advisable, however, for the older and more superior students to be asked to co-operate in the making out of test and examination questions, both of the objective and discussion type. Such a committee may also be given general diagnostic duties: to determine topics or questions poorly learned, items requiring review or drill, and the students who need individual advice, encouragement, or help. Such findings can be of assistance to the program committee and will probably furnish a teacher with some helpful illumination as to difficulties from the students' point of view. If a testing committee is appointed, some interesting experiments may also be made in giving them the responsibility for inculcating and promoting an honor spirit in the class tests and examinations.

The school relations committee.—This committee may be thought of, in a general way, as having charge of the "foreign affairs" of the class—relations to the administration, to other rooms, and to the community. Visits to and from other classes in shared programs, the school or administrative bulletin, announcements or articles selected for the school paper, announcements of school activities, communications with other schools, and the arrangements of all community activities in which the class as such is to participate—all these may properly be conceived as functions of such a committee.

The music committee.—This committee and the next will have important functions only if music and art are part of a correlated or integrating course in the social studies, as is very commonly done in the progressive ex-

periments, especially in the junior high schools. Its duties
will then center largely around the correlation of content
in music and art with the related periods in history or
sections in geography. The committee will plan programs
dealing with the history of music, lives of great musi-
cians, the story of the origin of national anthems and
other music, and the folk songs as illustrations of phases
of our national life. Some co-operation with the music
department will have to be planned to bring about timely
correlations of both appreciation and singing lessons with
the proper social studies background.

The art committee.—This committee will have some
duties similar to those of the music committee in planning programs or topics that correlate painting, sculp-
ture, and architecture with historical, social, or geographic
backgrounds and origins, especially for great pictures or
buildings and famous artists. In this connection co-operation with the art department will be necessary to plan
correlations in art appreciation and in the fine arts with
the expressions of the life and spirit of their own times.
The field of architecture will be especially rich for students of American history when correlated with the study
of Mayan, Aztec, and Pueblo architecture, the Spanish
and Mediterranean styles of the southwest, the Colonial
and English of the East and South, and the skyscraper
and other phases of modern architecture as related to
urban congestion.

In addition to such program elements, the art committee may be given responsibilities in connection with the
room decorations, especially in supplying good reproductions of famous paintings or pictures of famous buildings for the room bulletin board. If the socializing method
is combined with activities of the laboratory type, to be
discussed in the next chapter, this committee will also
have important duties in the matter of planning visits to

art galleries and the drawing of maps, cartoons, charts, and illustrations of the social studies materials.

Special committees.—It may often be necessary to select special committees for some particular activity such as a field trip, a debate, dramatizations, oratorical or essay contests, or to co-operate with other departments on some of the construction projects.

Committee of the whole.—This method of class organization may be used as a desirable parliamentary experience on special occasions. It will be advisable to introduce the class to the technique of this procedure at the beginning of the semester and to have a frank understanding with them as to the degree of democratic control over class management and methods that is being turned over to their responsibility. Such planning will at least include the method of choosing class leaders and the procedure in selecting and changing committees. The class as a committee of the whole should also discuss, formulate, and determine the general duties of all important committees and decide methods, objectives, and procedures for class management directly or through their representatives. Some control, or at least power of conference and advice, should be given the class as to the amount of work to be covered in units, activities, or specific periods, and to consider and criticize the plans or programs of any committee if these are not succeeding or if they do not interest. It may also be considered advisable to experiment with giving the class authority to consider, as a committee of the whole, serious breaches of discipline and to decide openly on suitable correction or punishment.

Evaluation of committee management.—The whole purpose of such a plan of socialized management is to give the students important socializing experiences, to teach them the responsibility of co-operation in a group, as representatives, as executives, as citizens, engaged in

a self-governing enterprise for their own welfare. Each
has the opportunity to function as a group leader and
thus to learn his capacities and limitations for leadership
by experience and by social observation and criticism.
Each learns to plan ahead for the interests of the
group as well as for his own success; to co-operate in the
committees in give-and-take compromise; to accept suggestion and criticism from his associates, sometimes of
the frankest and most searching sort; to make him overcome all sorts of obstacles in making his plans work, even
the indifference or opposition of those for whom he is
planning; to make him feel conscious of what the whole
group wants and to try to achieve it as the group's chosen
representative. The force and necessity of majority rule
is learned by experience—the radical individualist is compelled to fit into the mass, into what the average society
needs and wants. The main objective is social growth, not
the memorization of facts, not the achievement of
teacher-determined grades. The socializing plan tries primarily to create an elementary situation which pupils
must meet in community life and to teach them by analogous experience the responsibilities of society.

From the point of view of pedagogical method and the
psychology of learning, in distinction from these social
aims, it may be added that the socialized program arises
out of the new progressive philosophy of education that
insists on interest induced by self-initiated activities recognized as truly purposeful. The class learning activity is
now the enterprise of their own community. Group objectives are substituted for teacher compulsion, pupil needs
for adult initiative and approach. The learning process
is seen through the eye of adolescent psychology in action. The student is induced to learn by doing things for
himself and for his group. The needs of the situation will
stimulate him to quick thinking when his plans bog down

and, in a surprising way, to original creative thinking that will contrast with the indifference or nonchalance with which he usually meets the preconceived plans imposed by the adult. The socialized plan will induce natural, fearless expression in contrast to the silence of disinterest and the repression of academically toned requirements.

The results of such a socialized program are not measurable. In fact, by objective tests on factual attainments, such a program may reveal irregular, specialized, unequally distributed achievements in information, with even important lapses that might shame or distress the formal teacher who insists on a carefully distributed learning emphasis on "essentials." On the basis of experience with such a socialized experiment, however, we might claim, and do claim, that the progressive method achieves results that may reasonably be balanced against irregularities in factual mastery.

Practical suggestions for socialized management.—A few miscellaneous suggestions may be added about details of the committee plan for class management.

The teacher must support all actions of committees, especially the program committee's plans and assignments. If errors are recognized, the committee should be corrected and advised in private after the class.

The class chairman should be instructed to recognize volunteer impromptu contributions by members of the class. Some of the best contributions of personal experiences cannot be anticipated in committee programs or in the teacher's plans, but should, nevertheless, be permitted and encouraged.

Opportunity must be given all class members, however, to express their criticisms of committee plans and actions and to offer constructive suggestions for improvements in the class management. This may best be done by having it definitely understood that all such criticisms and suggestions should be written carefully and handed to the teacher or to the chairman of the committee concerned.

SOCIALIZING STUDY AND RECITATIONS

Co-operative study.—There are two distinct phases to socialized learning: co-operative study and group discussion of common learning problems. For the latter a conventionalized term, "the socialized recitation," has come into common use. For the former, which has not become so definitely identified as a learning technique, the topic chosen for this section, co-operative study, is sufficiently descriptive.

Co-operative study may involve the working together of all members of the class or of several students engaged in a learning enterprise in a smaller group, the class being divided into a number of such co-operative groups. Either of these is naturally suited to social studies materials, especially if the teacher, in a somewhat conservative spirit, feels that all members of the class should have a common textbook background of information and prefers a more intensive emphasis on certain elements than students might gather from the rapid introductory reading for perspective that has been recommended in our earlier discussion of the unit plan. Such intensive, co-operative study, largely for purposes of assignment, evaluation, or review, is directed by the teacher, with all students, with textbooks open, following his discussion and directions. The teacher's activity may be of the semi-lecture type of explanatory and evaluating purpose. The students' activities are of three sorts: reading indicated sentences or paragraphs; finding answers to thought-provoking questions; or interrupting with questions or volunteer contributions if the discussion is conducted in a truly co-operative spirit. The teacher promotes the progress of their common enterprise by pointing out the important topics, tracing movements and cause-and-effect relations of events; by asking or answering questions or referring them to other students; by challenging explanatory clarification or restatement of difficult or significant elements; and by presenting as rich an offering of supplementary information as his larger resources may suggest. Throughout, there must be a clear understanding in the class that all this activity, even the teacher's questioning, is study and study guidance, and in no sense testing or recitation.

In the small-group co-operative study, a variety of combinations and uses is apparent. Some of these activities are involved in the committee plans suggested in the previous general section. Other arrangements, similar in organization and execution, may be made directly by the teacher if the socialized class management is not included in the general plans. The small-group co-operative study arrangement is feasible in varying degrees in such study activities as the collection of illustrative or collateral materials, in the preparation of maps, charts, or other construction work, in library research assignments, in the composition and acting of dramatizations, in the responsibility for preparation and reports on current events, in the making of scrapbooks and picture portfolios, or in field trips to places where visits by the whole class are not feasible. Only one or two groups may be assigned to meet for a co-operative contribution, or the whole class may be constantly at work in the grouped way, with a regularly shifting personnel in the different groups. This small-group co-operative method is a common and important feature of much of the activity program now found so commonly in progressive elementary schools.

In arranging the problems for the small co-operative study groups, topics and activities must be assigned that will promote and hold group interest. The motivation of serious and progressive work is no easy matter to achieve in such a study plan, but the co-operative and social contributory appeal, as well as the intrinsic interest of the task itself, must be thoughtfully anticipated.

In selecting the personnel of groups, variations in ability and the presence of leadership must be kept in mind. The technique of such small-group co-operation as a social method commonly resorted to as a means of efficient transaction of business must be clearly understood by the class and can be given preliminary explanation and illustration by showing how Congress or other parliamentary organizations accomplish most of their business by this delegation of activities to selected committees. All these precautions are essential to prevent the small study group from degenerating into an opportunity for idling and futile waste of study time. Supervision by the teacher of small group activity and a social accounting for results to the whole class must be used to re-enforce a serious attitude in all such study enterprises.

Socialized recitation.—Because of the nature of the subject matter, the social studies present the most successful field for the use of the socialized recitation. This statement must not be understood in reverse order—the socialized recitation is not necessarily the most desirable type of class period for all work in history and civics. The use of such a period is advised only occasionally, but it is recommended especially in connection with reviews or with class discussions of topics and problems for which all students have had ample opportunity for study. The socialized recitation must be fundamentally understood to be a mode of student expression.

The general technique of the socialized recitation involves the following salient features:

1. Guidance of a discussion under the leadership of a student chairman.

2. Specific materials presented by a few leaders, usually as directed or planned by a student program committee.
3. A common background of information familiar to all members of the class.
4. Free, random, informal, but courteous discussion of ideas or questions presented by pupil program committee, discussion leaders, or chairman.
5. Occasional interruptions by the teacher to control and direct the pupil discussion.

Necessary conditions for socialized discussion.—In order to achieve the full values of the socialized recitation or discussion one must keep clearly in mind the chief purpose of the method. This is to give students certain important socializing experiences that are rarely acquired as purposeful training in school and can be attained in real life only by those who have the good fortune of an exceptional social environment at home. This is the training in the art of conversation in a group of some size, where courteous listening and generous but pertinent participation are essential skills in a worthy social development. The size of the typical school class is not so large but that the socialized discussion makes possible the nearest, and often the only, approach to training in the art of general group conversation that most young people will encounter. The average class group is as suitable for this as it is for the experience of addressing an audience. The student is entitled to have both these social expression experiences in his high school years. The average class is not too small for the one, nor too large for the other.

There is no body of subject matter that is so appropriate for such exercises in social discussion as the social sciences. The topics of common interest and conversation

in adult circles lie largely in this field, and the occasions
for use of this social art also lie largely in the field of current political and civic events. There is, therefore, no
artificial strain in urging the special use of this method in
these subjects.

Some practical suggestions.—Some further general suggestions in connection with the use of this method may be
given in summary form:

1. Teachers must recognize the difficulties, limitations, and possible failings with pupil leadership.
Selection of a presiding chairman or program committee chairman should be kept in the teacher's control or at least be subject to strong teacher suggestion.
If a socialized recitation begins to lag because of the
inability of the chairman, the teacher should feel
free to substitute another or to abandon the discussion by that method for the day.

2. In the truly socialized recitation the activities
will depart considerably from the typical audience
situation that is characteristic of the topical recitation method. There is a larger degree of informality; in fact, the discussion is free-for-all, limited only
by courtesy and the desire to avoid the confusion
resulting from several trying to talk at the same time
or from having the class discussion break up into
small group discussions.

3. The most important occasion for interference
by the teacher will be to prevent discussions from
being sidetracked too widely or frequently from the
main topic. Some tangents, however, are wholesome
and more worth while than the academic background
from which they diverge.

4. Pupils should be instructed in the development
of typical thought-questions. The technique of

"how" and "why" questions should be explained directly to the class in connection with the socialized recitation. Further understanding of the use of such questions should come about by the example of the teacher in proposing problems of the thought-provoking type.

5. Students who have secured the attention of the group should be allowed to finish their line of thought. Discourteous interruptions by other students or impatient interference by the teacher should be avoided as far as possible. One should never lose sight of the fact that the chief purpose of the socialized recitation is to give training in expression.

6. A considerable amount of collateral reading is helpful in making a success of a socialized recitation. This period can be used to give those who have done outside reading a chance to make contributions. It is also a period intended to give additional information to other members of the class. In this respect the values of this method make it comparable to a topical recitation.

7. In the planning of socialized recitations it will be advisable to deal only with large units. Free discussion, with any considerable number of the class taking part, can hardly be expected if the topic is narrow or detailed.

8. In classes that are not sectioned on the basis of abilities it will require some ingenuity on the part of the teacher to keep bright students or those who are forward in controversy from monopolizing too much of the discussion.

9. A blackboard outline of the unit under discussion will help considerably in preventing wandering and unbalanced emphasis.

SOCIALIZING ACTIVITIES AND EXPERIENCES

Real-life socializing activities.—In addition to treating the typical classroom learning processes in a socializing spirit there are a number of obvious school and community activities that may properly be considered as extracurricular, but are so charged with possibilities for training in good citizenship and general social efficiency that they may most properly be thought of as finding their initiative and inspiration in the social studies classroom. Some of these may originate in the general school administration, especially if there is a strong element of student participation in the school government. It is not advocated here that the social studies teacher should assume the prerogatives of the principal's office in such plans, but rather that the social studies classes, as such, may properly be considered as the most likely groups for co-operation in such activities or that they may reasonably display a supplementary initiative to enrich the school's service to the community. Such co-operation and initiative are urged as worthy enterprises of social studies classes because the experiences incidental to most of these community and civic activities involve an educative motivation for, or application of, the spirit and materials of the social science classwork.

An illustrative list of some of these socializing experiences will suggest the possibilities of participation in real-life activities:

Attending political meetings
Taking part in "drives"
Making posters for school or community enterprises
Speaking at public meetings
Civic or citizenship projects
Promoting and participating in civic oratorical contests

Pageants and plays for school and community
Writing community history
Writing school news for local newspapers
Directing traffic on big community days
Acting as hosts and guides and ushers to visiting
    groups
Selling tickets for local lectures or concerts
Co-operating with service clubs
Co-operating with the Red Cross in emergencies
Serving elementary schools in athletic contests
Serving on safety committees in school
Serving as traffic police
Promoting beauty and cleanliness of school grounds
Sponsoring school or community parties
Co-operating with the Parent-Teachers Association

Amateur citizenship.—Students get an adequate opportunity in school days to acquire the descriptive information about political and social institutions and civic machinery and to gain experience in classroom and general
school activities of some of the practices that can be used
in adult community action. There is a field of practice,
however, suggested in the foregoing list of activities that
will offer a nearer approach to reality than the common
academic training involved in either textbook information or extracurricular analogies. There is an intermediate realm between these learning experiences and the
adult's actual civic enterprises. This intermediate field
may be thought of as that of amateur citizenship, indirectly connected with the civic pursuits of the mature and
involving the possibilities of considerable helpful contribution to the communal welfare as well as a worthy
opportunity for practice in real civic service. This is a
field that has too commonly been overlooked by the
schools, especially for those high school students who

possess abilities and attitudes that qualify them for such
co-operative service. Without imposing partisan views or
bias the social studies teacher may even be expected to
promote or encourage political activities that will give
training in civic experiences. Let the student determine
his own political affiliations or be determined by the influence of home preferences, he may still be encouraged
to try his hand at such political activities in an election
campaign as canvassing; distributing literature in be-
half of preferred parties or candidates; making posters to
be displayed in local store windows; or preparing and, if
ability warrants and opportunity offers, delivering
speeches for political meetings. In local contests there is
no reason why an impartial program, in the nature of a
debate or a series of separate speeches by students, presenting all sides of an issue or an election contest, may
not be planned by the amateur citizens for the enlighten-
ment or judgment of their elders. Such humble duties as
attendance at political meetings and a critical discussion
of the campaign orators can be required of all prospective
citizens.

This explicit discussion of a few such civic activities,
selected at random from the list above, should be sufficient to show the possibilities of promoting projects, ap-
proximating or realizing adult civic or political duties, in
the intermediate field of amateur activities. One need
only take a second glance at the list to realize that the
possibilities of directing student energy into experiences
that will offer valuable training and strongly promote
proper social attitudes are even more feasible in many
lines of nonpolitical community service. For many of
these services it is difficult enough to get adequate adult
co-operation because of occupational demands. The direction of amateur citizenship into organized co-operation
in community enterprises that involve no partisan con-

flict can win only the most generous appreciation for one's school. Initiative in such social service could nowhere more reasonably be expected than in the social studies classes.

BIBLIOGRAPHY

Fancler, D. G., and Crawford, C. C.: *Teaching the Social Studies.* Los Angeles: C. C. Crawford, University of Southern California, 1933.

Hatch, R. W.: *Training in Citizenship.* New York: Charles Scribner's Sons, 1926, Chapter XV.

Klapper, Paul: *The Teaching of History.* New York: D. Appleton-Century Company, 1926.

Knowlton, Daniel C.: *History and the Other Social Studies in the Junior High School.* Charles Scribner's Sons, 1926.

Robbins, C. L.: *The Socialized Recitation.* Boston: Allyn & Bacon, 1920.

Sandwick, R. L.: *How and What to Study.* Boston: D. C. Heath & Company, 1915.

Sheffield, A. D.: *Creative Discussion.* (Second Edition) New York: Association Press, 1931.

Stormzand, M. J.: *Progressive Methods of Teaching.* Boston: Houghton Mifflin Company, 1924, Chapter X.

Tryon, R. M.: *The Teaching of History in Junior and Senior High Schools.* Boston: Ginn & Company, 1921.

PERIODICALS

Chase, L. S., and Clark, M. G.: "Social Studies as Life Experiences." *Junior-Senior High School Clearing House,* October, 1930, pp. 102-109.

Mackie, R. A.: "The Socialized Recitation." *Historical Outlook,* January, 1928, pp. 34-35.

Zimmerman, R.: "Working Plan of Teaching How to Study." *Educational Review,* October, 1927, pp. 168-171.

CHAPTER V

LABORATORY METHOD AND VISUAL AIDS

Basic elements in laboratory method.—There are two basic conditions in conducting a social studies class by the laboratory method. These may be inferred by analogy from the way laboratory work is done in the teaching of science. The two basic elements are the organization of work as *supervised study,* highly individualized, and the provision of *special equipment* suitable for the activities involved.

As a corollary to these basic principles it must be recognized, however, that the laboratory method should be thought of, not as a distinctive, exclusive method of procedure, but as a possible supplement or variation of the other general programs described in this book. The social studies laboratory may even be combined with the traditional textbook recitation procedure. The term, therefore, may be understood as a comprehensive one to include a number of miscellaneous devices and activities which are intended to give the study of history, geography, and civics certain concrete, real, and vitally active elements.

The name "laboratory method" has been urged by those who are anxious to promote a large element of constructive work or other activities in the social studies program.

Typical activities in the social studies laboratory.— This explanation may be given a more concrete form by simply listing a number of the typical activities that are characteristic of a social studies classroom motivated by the laboratory spirit. Such a list would include the following:

1. The study and making of maps
2. Outlining, summarizing, and other notebook work
3. Individual study of research topics
4. Fact-finding from reference books
5. The consultation of source books
6. Self-testing by the students, with such study guide tests or workbooks as were described in Chapter II
7. The making of models, drawings, and realia
8. The making of pictures and cartoons
9. Examination of atlases and globes by individual students in connection with their study
10. The making of tables, charts, and graphs
11. The making and showing of camera slides with the stereopticon lantern
12. The showing of motion pictures or similar helps supplied by the visual education departments in large city schools or by the extension departments of many of the state universities
13. Field trips to museums, or other places of historical interest
14. Field trips to civic and governmental institutions
15. Collecting pictures and making picture portfolios or scrapbooks
16. Making illustrated problem or topic books
17. Dramatization, including composition and presentation
18. Surveys of local conditions

This list of laboratory work is here given without implied advice as to the use of all items. Some of these typical activities are here included with considerable reservations as to their value. Specific difficulties will be noted in subsequent sections.

Fundamental plans and organization.—We may now return to the discussion of the basic elements in the method, dealing first with the class organization for study. The content of a course conducted by the laboratory method may range from the very conventional text-book course to the more informal progressive plans outlined in detail in other chapters of this book.

In any case the assumption is that the class period shall be largely given over to "work," not to a testing recitation which assumes that the study preparations of the class must be made at home or in a study hall at some other time. In short, as was stated at the outset, the laboratory method requires, as a basic feature, a large element of supervised study during the class period—students are to do their learning in large part, if not entirely, during the class period scheduled for that subject. Any teacher who has a theory of social studies work opposed to this fundamental organization should not attempt the laboratory method except for very occasional activities.

Supervised study and study methods.—The ideal arrangement of a high school schedule should provide for full hour class periods. With this much time available, at least one half of the time should be given to the students for study during the class period, if the laboratory method is to be the basic plan of class organization. An even larger proportion for study and work is feasible and advisable.

In connection with this advice it is necessary to point out that all supervised study need not be silent, individual study on the part of the pupil. A large proportion of the time can be given to the type of work that has been described as the discussion method or may be thought of as directed oral co-operative study.

The individual, silent study of assignments or of collateral reading should give the teacher occasion for teaching pupils how to study history, or whatever the subject may be, and for helping them to get a definite understanding of specific study methods. Teachers should familiarize themselves with the general discussions on study methods in the manuals available.

Some of the study methods which could be taught high school students in connection with history or other social studies are the following:

(1) Rapid silent reading, or skimming: This is perhaps the most important and significant for all purposes during the high school years, but nowhere is it more significant than in such subjects as history and literature, where large supplementary assignments are desirable. Such rapid reading is essential in history work for several purposes. The most important, of course, is the gathering of material that covers topics not included in the regular text. Another purpose is the comparison of different points of view in various accounts. Still another is the skimming to get specific information on particular facts or topics. Such rapid reading of the textbook is equally important for the perspective study advised in connection with the unit plan.

(2) Use of the index and table of contents: The independent use of these methods for getting outline perspectives and the relation of facts or events chronologically separated should be taught by class practice, both in the textbook and in other books developed on a more extended plan.

(3) Preparation for class discussion on problem questions: Many of the problem questions for class thinking and discussion given in the textbooks may be used for the discussion period in connection with the advance assignments, but others of these questions will involve consid-

erable work in comparison and cross-reference reading in other parts of the text, and in some cases in comparison with other textbooks or supplementary assignments. Other questions in these lists involve a thinking reaction on the part of the student in dealing with facts previously acquired, or in making cause-and-effect or other deductions from the materials. In this connection the students should be made conscious of the technique of reflection or thinking about their reading. All of this has in mind a more formal selection of problems more directly related to a basic textbook than the problem-solving technique discussed in Chapter III in connection with present-day issues and the use of current events as an organizing principle for a correlated social studies course. The explanations of the problem method given there are, however, equally applicable to the more conventional course assumed here.

(4) Intensive reading: Careful reading, in contrast to skimming for perspective, need not be thought of as slow reading, but rather as thoughtful perusal for some specific purpose. Such purposes may include the search for specific facts or important details, the tracing of cause-and-effect relations, the visualizing of events, the meaning or use in context of particular words, thoughtful doubting or challenge, the detection of a partisan or prejudiced point of view, the application or illustration of history or civics elements in present-day events or problems, the discovery of paragraph topics, or other forms of concentration for permanent learning of important elements for retention.

(5) Outlining or summarizing: These two related study methods are among the most common in all content subjects such as the social sciences. Both methods include a conscious evaluation of the relative importance of facts or sentences in a paragraph, or of paragraphs in

a larger section. The outlining usually results in a written topical analysis showing the logical divisions and subdivisions with careful determination of co-ordination and subordination in the relation of topics. In the summary complete sentence statements are formulated for the condensation of a paragraph thought, or a paragraph is written to combine and correlate the ideas of a section or chapter.

(6) Testing oneself on questions: Students should be trained to test themselves consciously and systematically on their understanding or mastery of such questions as are provided on each chapter in a textbook or on such as the teacher may select or provide in connection with a study assignment. A variation of this method is the formulation of similar questions by the student himself on such elements in a reading assignment as he considers important or such as offer difficulties in comprehension.

Practical suggestions on supervised study.—A number of practical suggestions in connection with the use of supervised study may be briefly outlined:

1. Avoid wasting the supervised study time by certain busywork types of activity. Such concrete assignments as map and graph making are more appropriate for outside assignments.

2. Avoid interruptions of study periods. A program involving the division of a class period for supervised study or discussion, and for testing, should be strictly adhered to, at least as far as the time allotted for study is concerned. It is very easy for a teacher to be tempted to encroach upon the supervised study period for recitation purposes. This is distinctly unfair to the study methods. Practically the only interruptions that can be justified are the supervision of the work of individual students in

such a way as not to disturb the study of others or to give suggestions about study methods to the group as a whole when they seem to be needed.

3. In order to make supervised study in the social studies successful it will be necessary to make rather liberal provision for such reference study materials in the classroom as the school can afford. A judicious selection of reference books, including a standard encyclopedia, an atlas, individual dictionaries, a number of copies of parallel textbooks, and a select group of books for supplementary reading, should be readily accessible in the room.

4. Avoid confusing the pupil by attempting to teach too great a variety of study methods. It is more desirable for students to acquire the ability to use two or three specific methods in a semester than to have an indefinite notion about a larger number. The selection of particular study methods for emphasis with any class must rest in the judgment of the teacher.

5. The chief motive in making a student conscious of a variety of study methods is to make him increasingly independent in his future study. The teacher's ultimate goal here, it has been said, is to make himself unnecessary. This motive has been clearly defined in one of the recommendations of the American Historical Association's Commission on the Social Studies in urging that "the competent teacher, without evading a single iota of his responsibility as the guiding and directing force in the educative process, will be unalterably opposed to the doctrine that the pupil should be a passive recipient of his ministrations, an inert receptacle into which he is expected to pour the knowledge and wisdom of

the race through the pipe-lines of the written and spoken word. Knowing that real learning requires the active response and participation of the pupil and that the supreme goal of education . . . is the growth of an independent yet socially sensitive personality, he will strive continuously to develop in the child habits of independent study, inquiry, thought, and action and thus free him as quickly and completely as possible from reliance upon the formal and authoritarian tutelage of teacher, school, and elders. In particular he will endeavor to acquaint the pupil with diverse ideas and points of view and cultivate in him a reasoned scepticism regarding the claims advanced in support of any social doctrine or program." [1]

Reference or library work.—The use of a general library should be one of the study methods every student should acquire during the high school period. The responsibility for this is divided among several departments, but the principal obligation falls on the English and history groups. A number of school systems throughout the country are now arranging for a regular course in the use of the library, required of all students, and there are several manuals with suggestions for practical application that can be used to teach students the intelligent use of libraries. Teachers who are not familiar with the formal planning of such technique will find valuable detailed suggestions in any of the manuals dealing with the use of the library.

Outline for a library course.—A series of specific lessons for a library course, either in connection with social studies work or for a separate class, with responsibilities

---

[1] From *Conclusions and Recommendations*, pp. 82-83. Reprinted through the courtesy of Charles Scribner's Sons, New York.

divided between the librarian and the English and social studies departments, is given in outline, followed by a sample lesson for one of the topics to illustrate the method:

1. How libraries are usually arranged. (The American Library Association System.)
2. By what system is our school library arranged?
3. How to use a library card catalogue
4. How to find a book after you know the number
5. The *Readers' Guide,* and how to use it
6. *Who's Who in America;* how to use it
7. How to find a date for an event, or an event for a date
8. How to find statistics for geography, history, or civics—the use of the *World Almanac, Statesman's Year Book,* encyclopedias, and census reports and other government publications
9. How to use encyclopedias
10. How to use different elements of a dictionary
11. How to use synonym and antonym books
12. How to use books of quotations
13. How to make a bibliography, or brief reference list, for a topic or theme
14. How to find parallel accounts on a topic. (Review and combination of lessons on card catalogue and *Readers' Guide* along with use of Index and Table of Contents of books in proper section of library.)
15. How to find a book list or brief bibliography on a subject
16. How to take notes on your reading through quotations, outlines, and summaries of facts and ideas

A working lesson is offered for the first problem in the above list, as arranged by one of the authors in a course for junior high school classes in Santa Monica, California:

Lesson I. *How Libraries Are Generally Arranged.*
All books are divided into two sections:
   a. Fiction (invented story)
   b. Non-fiction

In the Dewey Decimal or American Library Association System all non-fiction books are divided into ten classes according to the subject they deal with. All books on the same subject will be together under the same class number. This number will be on the back of the book.

000-099 General Books   (as encyclopedias)
100-199 Philosophy   (vocation)
200-299 Religion   (mythology)
300-399 Sociology   (government, economics)
400-499 Language   (dictionaries, grammars in all languages)
500-599 Science   (chemistry, biology, etc.)
600-699 Useful Arts   (home economics, engineering, medicine)
700-799 Fine Arts   (painting, architecture, music, etc.)
800-899 Literature
900-999 History

Each of these classes is subdivided. After or below the call number comes a letter, as, 812F; the letter stands for the first letter of the author's name. Non-fiction books are arranged on the shelves numerically. All fiction books are arranged on the shelves alphabetically by author.

1. Would a novel by Kipling be found before or after a novel by Verne?
   Answer:

2. Under what class number would I find the Greek mythology books?
   Answer:

3. Under what class number would I find a book on the Civil War?
   Answer:

4. Under what class number would I find a dictionary?
   Answer:

5. Under what class number would I find an encyclopedia?
   Answer:

6. Under what class number would I find a book on music?
   Answer:

7. Under what class number would I find a Bible?
   Answer:

8. Under what class number would I find a Spanish book?
   Answer:

9. Under what class number would I find a book on radio?
   Answer:

10. Under what class number would I find a book on birds?
    Answer:

Suggestions as to library instruction.—A number of detailed practical suggestions may be given in connection with the teaching of library technique and the making of reports on collateral or supplementary reading in the social studies.

1. Where definite arrangements for teaching students the use of the library have not been made in the school course of study, the history teachers should try to get a co-operative understanding with the teachers of English as to the phases of library use to be taught the students in connection with specific courses, and in such a way as to provide for a division of the responsibility of each department for particular topics.

2. The history teacher should plan to familiarize all pupils with the social science section in the school library at the beginning of the course. Similar instructions should be made with reference to the social science sections in public libraries where this can be easily arranged. Students should be required to do this for themselves early in the course. In any school or public library all histories are arranged in a single section, while the books on civics, government, social problems, and geography are found in other sections. This American Library Association classification, as a characteristic of book arrangement in all up-to-date libraries in the country, should be understood by all high school students.

3. All history teachers should realize their responsibility for the systematic development of the social science sections in the school library. The development of many school libraries is largely a matter of chance. The responsibility for systematic additions with a proper distribution of acquisitions for various departments is not often recognized by the principal, the librarian, or department heads. New additions are made from year to year largely in pro-

portion to the initiative of individual teachers in requesting the purchase of particular books. As a result most school libraries are very unbalanced in their collections. It will, therefore, be the responsibility of the social studies teachers to see that the proper share of new books is added to the social science sections from year to year.

4. In addition to the use of the school and public libraries for collateral reading in the way of assignments or requirements in the course itself, social studies teachers should realize their duty to motivate the use of the libraries for general cultural or recreational reading. This applies especially to the use of biographical material, which students should be led to select as one of their leading recreational reading interests.

5. The most important library method to be taught high school students, not only for use in connection with social studies courses, but also for general education, is the use of the library card catalogue. The teacher should understand the standard method advised by the American Library Association and the Congressional Library and the modification or adaptation that may be made of this standard form in the local libraries. Both the standard form of card cataloguing and the method used in the school and city libraries available should be understood by all high school students. Exercises to test their understanding and ability to use the card catalogue should be planned early in the course.

6. As a background for the widest use of the library and the connection of the regular classwork to the libraries, students should be required to use some of the reference lists given in the textbook at

the end of each chapter, or similar reference lists that the teacher may choose to use.

7. Students should also be taught the distinctive values of all such standard reference works as are available in the local libraries. This will include all encyclopedia sets, *Who's Who, Who's Who in America, The Statesman's Year-Book, The World Almanac,* biographical dictionaries, and the special encyclopedias for the social studies.

8. In the larger school libraries, where back numbers or files of magazines are on the shelves, students should be taught the use of these magazine files through the *Readers' Guide.* All the details about the successive arrangement of this index to periodical literature, its relation to *Poole's Index,* and the cumulative annual and quarterly volumes should be understood. The technique of using the *Readers' Guide* should be taught by practical exercises as well as by explanation.

Teaching historical method.—One phase of library work to which the social studies teacher may give some attention, both for purposes of instruction and self-development, may be designated as the learning of "historical method." The comparison of conflicting authorities and the earliest contact with source books will open the door to this significant technique of the student of history. Unless he has had a special university course along these lines, some study of the science or method of history research and history writing should prove of great value to the teacher. There is a specialized technique, fully developed, for dealing with sources and evaluating testimony and documents, for the purposes of detecting misinformation and determining reliability, a technique that the teacher of social studies will find especially necessary when he attempts to interpret recent or current events.

The duty of attaining proficiency in this science of history and of making a beginning of imparting the technique and its spirit to all prospective citizens has been urged as a paramount obligation by the American Historical Association's Commission on the Social Studies. In its recent Report, this group of leaders declares that "the competent teacher will strive to emulate, even though his powers be relatively feeble, the methods of great thinkers and teachers of all ages—will become acquainted with the classics and fundamental works in the given field, will know how to use bibliographical and library apparatus in the acquisition of knowledge, will know how to apply the engines of scholarly criticism, verification, and authentication to facts true and alleged, will know how to analyze complicated documents and social situations, will know how to take and weigh testimony by the judicial process, will know how to observe the occurrences and participate in the life of the neighborhood, will illustrate these procedures in classroom and community, and by precept and example will strive to transfer his powers to his pupils. Above all, the competent teacher should know thoroughly the subject matter which he professes to teach, should see its relation to the life of mankind, and should have an infectious enthusiasm about it—to this, all teaching methods are subordinate." [2]

Room equipment for laboratory work.—In general it may be said that the ideal social studies room for the laboratory method will be a combination of library and workshop. In the sections dealing with library lessons it has been assumed that most of this work will have to be done in the general school library, as this is the present

[2] In *Conclusions and Recommendations*, pp. 83-84.

condition in most schools. In an ideal situation, however, social studies rooms as well as English rooms will have to be decidedly modified to make possible more efficient study plans and to accommodate the needs of students and teachers working with the progressive methods that are dealt with in this book.

Every social studies room should be equipped with some of the reference materials referred to in the library course: a big dictionary, at least one encyclopedia set, an atlas, a number of reference books such as the *World Almanac, Who's Who in America,* a book of dates such as Ploetz's *Epitome,* a *Statesman's Year-Book,* and a copy of the summary volume of the last census. A room library should also contain copies of a number of different textbooks parallel to the basic text, if one is used, or a collection of such texts, in sets of a half-dozen each, in sufficient total to supply each member of the class. A few simpler as well as a few more advanced textbooks than those specially suited for the grade should be included in the collection.

Besides such textbooks a more varied social studies room library should be available, with at least one or two hundred selected books. Good lists for this purpose are given in appendices in a number of the leading high school or college textbooks.

In addition to the library equipment, it seems advisable to have available, for some of the other laboratory activities described in this chapter, as much of the following equipment as the school can afford to furnish:

A globe
Atlas and wall maps
Several drawing boards and sets of mechanical draw-
ing instruments
Materials for freehand drawing and water colors

Scissors, paste, crayons, colored chalks
Various sorts of cross-section charting paper
A manual training workbench and tools
Sewing machine and sewing table
Piano
Collections of folk songs
Phonograph and records
Radio with short-wave length attachment
Typewriter
A mimeographing apparatus
Bookbinding equipment
Telegraph instruments
Rubber-stamp lettering outfit
Motion-picture projection machine
Motion-picture camera
Stereopticon camera
Material to make stereopticon slides
A dark room for developing films
Scrapbooks for cartoons and pictures
Material for making scrapbooks
A portfolio of famous historical pictures
Newspapers and magazines
A filing case
Adequate bulletin board space
Swinging display boards
First-aid equipment
Stamp catalogue
Postcard albums for historical and travel scenes

This list of equipment and materials is an idealistic composite of what a number of progressive teachers report as provided for their programs. Not even the most enthusiastic innovator could hope to get all of such an ideal outfit from the most extravagant school board. Many of the most expensive items are traditionally reserved for the shops and laboratories of other departments, and the use of such apparatus can be secured only by generous co-operation. Other items included in the list for social studies work may seem fanciful to those who do not realize the degree to which laboratory activities have been developed in these subjects.

OTHER TYPES OF LABORATORY WORK

In addition to the supervised study and library instruction there are four distinct types of student activity that may be grouped under the laboratory plan.

Construction work.—Most important of these are various sorts of construction work, resulting in certain products to illustrate or vivify the reading materials, that are usually productive of interested motivation for the research necessary for their proper execution. Included in this list of construction activities we find all sorts of map making; the drawing of charts and graphs; the making of models and other realia; costume designing and making costumes for models, pageants, or dramatizations; and the preparation of scrapbooks and picture portfolios. Other activities of this sort may be suggested by items in the list of equipment and materials given in the preceding section.

Preparing visual aids.—Another general type of laboratory work may be classified as the exhibition of visual aids and the preparation of materials for distinctive work of this sort. The operation of a stereopticon lantern can provide an endless variety of visual aids for all phases of social studies work, not only in the showing of slides that are available commercially or as loans from state universities, but to an unlimited degree in the reproduction of pictures, maps, and graphs that can be made with little labor and expense by students. These may be reproduced from books by a very simple copying process, and

desirable diagrams and charts can thus be made available
for the whole class. Similar apparatus can be secured for
such reproductions, or for original pictures, with some of
the simpler moving-picture outfits. Both cameras and
projectors, as well as the reproduction apparatus, involve a comparatively slight cost. The films available in
commercial moving pictures of standard size are still too
limited in number and are mostly of such slight educational merit that the more expensive projectors are hardly
justified for most high schools.

Music appreciation.—A third type of laboratory work,
the production or appreciation of such music as the patriotic, regional, or folk songs, may find some basis for
classification in social studies laboratory activities, especially in those broader integrating courses where free
correlations are attempted. Instrumental production of
such illustrative materials will involve either a generous
co-operation with the music department or the use of
piano, phonograph, or radio in the classroom.

Written composition.—All forms of original expression
should also be considered as phases of the laboratory
plan, especially if the composition involved is executed
in the classroom under sympathetic direction of the
teacher. Essays, stories, poems, imaginary diaries and
letters, plays, pageants, cartoons, and illustrations, dealing directly with the social studies materials and intended for class, home, school, or community presentation, will comprise a large part of the laboratory activities. Content and motivation for these types of expression, which are generally thought of as properties of other
departments, may most successfully be naturalized as
integrated activities in social studies classes. Dramatization should not be understood in too restricted a sense.
It is not to be confined to the more ambitious efforts of
playwrighting and acting or to the elaborate forms of pa-

geantry. Imaginative, vicarious experiences of the struggles in thought and action of those who engaged in the building of the nation, in the settlement of the continent, and in the creation of its institutions and ideals can be felt and understood by students of today in a variety of composition exercises. These may vary from simpler forms of expression suitable for the grades to the more ambitious undertakings of high school students, involving considerable research and imaginative ingenuity. A variety of such devices is suggested in the Report of the Commission on the Social Studies of the American Historical Association. It declares that "the competent teacher, without substituting a fictitious world for the reality, will encourage the pupil to make imaginary journeys, draw imaginary pictures and diagrams, write imaginary letters, diaries and autobiographies, engage in imaginary debates and participate in various forms of dramatization." [3] In connection with all such dramatic and imaginative exercises it is advisable to heed the caution implied in the phrase, "without substituting a fictitious world for the reality." These are not to be free inventions but truly reproductive as far as the study of contemporary sources and reliable descriptions can bring back the true circumstances of local color, costume, character, events, and even the language used.

Field trips.—Similarly from the natural sciences the social subjects have borrowed the idea and methods of excursions and field trips. Explorations with motives of general social experience and training constituted one of the conspicuous elements in the reformed programs of German schools under the Republic. So prominent did these educational excursions become that they were imitated by adult groups for social experience no less than for recreation. Field trips during vacation weeks, care-

[3] *Op. cit.*, p. 79.

fully prepared for by advance instruction and evaluated in the schools as a part of the regular work after their return, were included in the programs of many of the schools. In our own country we have become familiar with similar educative experiences made available on some of the Boy Scout outings. A more general adaptation of such education, with supervised observation of museums, galleries, other schools, governmental buildings and assemblies, industrial institutions, historical monuments, public works projects, and the like, is certain to be found in progressive social studies classes in the near future.

INDIVIDUAL DIFFERENTIATION IN ACTIVITIES

In order to adjust the work to students of varying capacities and interests two general principles must be kept in mind in all of these various forms of laboratory activity.

Each student should be directed into a variety of activities. One who does well in manual construction must not be encouraged to devote all his time to the making of models. He may be allowed to distinguish himself in some conspicuous project, but should not be permitted to convert his social studies course every day into another period for manual training. Costume making may have a similar fascination for some of the girls in a class, but the work here is not to be motivated as a supplementary training in the domestic arts to the detriment of the social studies content.

Yet no student should be forced into activities for which he has no special interest or capacity. A large enough variety of activities is available to avoid monotony or specialization on the one hand, and burdensome or inept execution on the other, from which the student can derive no satisfaction or pride as an expression of interest or as a contribution to the co-operative enterprises of the group.

This adaptation of classwork to immediate individual needs, interests, and experiences, in order to give it reality, is urged in the Report of the Commission on the Social Studies of the American Historical Association:

"The competent teacher, in an effort to keep his instruction in touch with living reality, will make full use of the class group—its diverse personalities, its differences in talent, its varied experiences, its conflicts of interests, its collective life; will relate his work so far as possible, to the organized life of the school as manifested in social activities, student groupings, and school government; and will regard the surrounding community as his social laboratory, utilizing its life and happenings and moving out through the normal avenues of communication—the press, the movie, and the radio—to observe and appraise the more important events in the nation and the world." [4]

The Commission's emphasis on the values of the student's interests and experiences in his school and community life, as vitalizing and giving the motivation of reality to his study of the social sciences, is not to be overlooked.

BIBLIOGRAPHY

Baldwin, J. W.: *The Social Studies Laboratory*. New York: Bureau of Publications, Teachers College, Columbia University, 1929.

Collings, Ellsworth: *Progressive Teaching in Secondary Schools*. Indianapolis: Bobbs Merrill Company, 1931, Chapters XVII and XVIII.

Crawford, C. C., and McDonald, L. P.: *Modern Methods in Teaching Geography*. Boston: Houghton Mifflin Company, 1929, Chapters VIII-X.

[4] In *Conclusions and Recommendations*, p. 80.

Dawson, Edgar: *Teaching the Social Studies.* New York: The Macmillan Company, 1927, Chapter XIV.

Johnson, Henry: *The Teaching of History in Elementary and Secondary Schools.* New York: The Macmillan Company, 1920, Chapters VIII-X.

Knowlton, Daniel C.: *History and tho Othor Social Studies in the Junior High School.* New York: Charles Scribner's Sons, 1926, Chapters III, V.

—— *Making History Graphic.* New York: Charles Scribner's Sons, 1925.

Rice, O. S.: *Lessons on the Use of Books and Libraries.* Chicago: Rand McNally & Company, 1920.

Simpson, Mabel E.: *Supervised Study in History.* New York: The Macmillan Company, 1924.

Stormzand, M. J.: *American History Teaching and Testing.* New York: The Macmillan Company, 1925.

PERIODICALS

Raetzer, E. Y.: "The Technique of Teaching History by the Laboratory Method in the History Department of the Trenton Senior High School." *Historical Outlook,* May, 1928, pp. 215-220.

Rugg, E. U.: "Supervised Study in History." *Historical Outlook,* April, 1920, pp. 142-149.

Wiberg, E., and Elston, B.: "Some Methods of Visualizing History." *Historical Outlook,* November, 1927, pp. 328-329.

Wilgus, A. C.: "The Laboratory Method in the Teaching and Studying of History." *Historical Outlook,* January, 1921, pp. 23-27.

Wilson, H. E., "Things to Do in the Social Science Classroom." *Historical Outlook,* May, 1929, pp. 218-224.

CHAPTER VI

INTEGRATING SOCIAL STUDIES AND ENGLISH

The meaning of integration.—In a meeting of progressive social studies teachers discussing "integration" it would soon become evident that this term is used in two distinct senses. Some would see the word as in the title of this chapter, implying the combination of two or more conventional school subjects into a single course. In this sense integration has reference to an extreme form of correlation of subject matter and processes, which, in the majority of schools, are still taught as separate subjects. The topical correlations of American history and civics, of the former, or of both subjects, with geography, have already been described under the unit plan in Chapter I. The correlation intended by the integration plan, however, goes beyond that. It is a combination of more than topical content. The completeness of the consolidation of several subjects into one becomes apparent at once when we think of combining any one of the social subjects with some subject not usually included in that group, as, for example, the typical senior high school course in American history and the course in American literature, or a course in civics with the subject of English composition. Such are typical integration experiments now being undertaken in some of the progressive schools.

Such a definition and description of integration would not be considered adequate, however, by many of the experimenting teachers and curriculum makers. They would prefer not to have integration defined in terms of subjects and content, not even in terms of methods of teaching or study. They look on integration as a purpose or objective; they insist on the child-centered point of view. Integration is something that happens to, or is done by, the student. The pupil integrates his history content and his composition activity in a learning act, in his interest, or in his understanding. In this sense integration comes close to the ideal of the unit-plan advocate when he speaks of a unit of interest, or of the "purposefulness" of the project, or of the self-initiated activity. There is the same implied criticism of the subject-minded, departmentalized specialist, the same opposition to the conventional observance of logically imposed dividing lines in content or processes or skills.

The point of view that is held throughout this chapter is that a pupil's learning experiences may be integrated to great educative advantage by some of the possible subject combinations that have been suggested above. Other integrating experiences might perhaps be found and will probably be tried out in experimental classes in the near future, in such combinations as English history and literature, first-year Latin and English, or English with such vocational courses as typewriting or printing. The integrating of American history and civics with English is discussed in detail partly because it seems to be one of the most feasible combinations, and partly because it has received considerable experimentation in recent practice.

The discussion of this plan has been left to the last in our list of new methods, not only because it is the most recent of the progressive teaching enterprises in the social studies, but also because it is the most radically advanced of the experiments that are attempting to give primary consideration to the pupil instead of to the school subjects.

The handicap of prejudice.—Throughout the chapter special advantages of this advanced method of integration will be urged. At the outset, therefore, it may seem to be the best place to point out several serious disadvantages that have to be met in attempting so important an innovation.

In the experiments that have been attempted in combining a semester's or a year's work in English with an equal assignment in the social sciences there is no intention or expectation of slighting either subject or of subordinating one to the other. It is therefore advised and assumed that students shall have the same amount of time for the combined course, the two full periods that would have been allowed if the subjects had been taken separately. This involves certain program and recording difficulties and, consequently, a probability of administrative opposition. Unless, then, the integrating method meets with administrative approval and sympathy, it cannot be successful.

But more serious still, in planning and executing the integration of social studies and English, teachers of the course have to contend with a serious handicap of departmental or subject-minded prejudice from other teachers and especially from department heads if these have any supervisory powers. If the teacher of the combined courses was formerly identified as a social studies teacher, it will be hard to avoid the suspicion and criticism of English-teaching associates. If the teacher is classified in the English department, the social science group will probably be critical. This is a natural, unavoidable result of the extreme specialization in preparation and interests demanded of teachers in the secondary schools. The reasonableness of such an extreme subject-minded attitude may well be questioned. No one will deny that a teacher who has majored in a subject in the university and who has had considerable experience in teaching it should be expected to do work in that field superior to the teacher who has had limited preparation and no special experience. Yet it is presuming altogether too much to claim that a good teacher of one of these subjects cannot teach high school students well in the other with a reasonable amount of conscientious preparation. It is true that a strongly subject-minded specialist in the social studies may justly be suspected of being likely to slight the English features in a consolidated course, and vice versa. It is not the strongly subject-minded teacher who should attempt or be intrusted with such an experiment in integration. The ideal teacher must have the child-centered point of view, he must be the teacher of youth, not of subjects. If, in addition, he has had a reasonable preparation and teaching experience in both subject fields, he should be above the prejudice of his too highly specialized associates.

Administration of integration or fusion courses.—Various forms of organization have been attempted in the experiments in integration. The description here must be confined to a comparison of the two most common forms. In either case we must assume the same class of pupils, of course, and a time allotment of two full class periods, preferably in immediate succession. The two plans differ in the arrangements for teaching. In one form, which we may call the co-operative, an English and a social studies teacher are assigned to the class to collaborate. In one arrangement of this form a class double the size of a typical class is assigned, say from fifty to seventy students, and both teachers are present and active for the double period. In the other variety of teacher co-operation, the class, of usual size, has one teacher one period, and the other a second period.

In the second general type of integration work one teacher has the full responsibility for all the work with a class for two periods and in both subjects. This last form is free from several serious objections that may be found in the two-teacher plan, for which the chief argument may be said to be the safeguarding of subject or departmental interests. The co-operative plan involves a great burden of personal adjustments in planning and execution, especially where the two teachers do not share all the educative experiences of the class. The exchange of reports and consultation about class activities involves a great extra load on the teachers' time and energy. Some of this co-operative burden may give the collaborating teachers an advantage over the one-teacher method. They must plan in great detail, and with great foresight, if they are expected to deal with prescribed limits of subject matter and activities in the combined fields. A sympathetic agreement on objectives, on eliminations, and on general unit divisions should be a matter of preliminary discussion. An agreeable division should be made as to certain skills and activities to be practiced in either the social studies class or the English class. Among these will be such matters as practice in reading, study methods, the preparation and delivery of oral reports, note taking, bibliography making, specific vocabulary expansion. The consultation may be burdensome, but it will have the advantage of mutual criticism or re-enforced agreement on values. The single teacher, solely responsible for the integration, has more freedom, but this freedom involves dangers of planlessness and lack of fair balance.

More difficult problems of an administrative nature are involved in some of the more ambitious integration plans in the junior high schools, where such subject consolidations of social studies and English may be extended to include projects or activities that involve work in shop construction, physical education, and especially in the art and music departments. Unless the whole school is organized in this freer plan, difficulties in teacher and pupil programs will be met and will have to be arranged and supervised carefully to avoid conflicts between the experimental and the conventional classes. Much of the necessary adjustment can be planned with due administrative foresight; further elements of conflict will have to be adjusted through experience.

The spirit and values of co-operation between teachers of different departments and subjects, the correlation of materials from different fields, in short the integration of the social studies with other branches is endorsed and advised in the Report of the Commission on Social Studies of the American Historical Association. In the section dealing with methods of teaching the social studies, the Commission declares that "the competent teacher, in order to improve the quality of his instruction, will seek to integrate his specialty with the work of his colleagues in the social sciences and with the total school curriculum—with instruction in literature, language, mathematics, natural science, and the arts." [1]

Vitalizing English work.—We may now turn to some of the arguments that are advanced in favor of the integration of work in English with the social studies. The most significant value probably lies in the vitalizing application of English work by giving it a social studies content and background. This claim is made for the literature as well as the composition phases, but especially for the latter. The argument here addresses itself especially to the criticism that is commonly made, and too often justified, that instruction in English is carried on in a vacuum.

In the study of literature the social background of the content, necessary for the most important phases of appreciation, is either neglected, or taken for granted, or has to be built up at a considerable sacrifice of time. A carefully planned co-ordination of the readings in Amer-

[1] In *Conclusions and Recommendations*, pp. 79-80.

ican literature with the period in history in which the content has its setting may reasonably be expected to integrate the pupil's understanding and interest, not only for his literary appreciation but for his broader grasp of the movements in history. The integrating values are fairly claimed to be reciprocal. The study of history can profit as much by having the student realize that the intellectual and aesthetic products of any period are more significant elements than the political or military events which the historian has generally chosen for exaggerated emphasis in the school textbooks.

In this connection it seems proper to point out that, in planning a consolidated course in these two subjects, the correlation should be made on the basis of the content of the piece of literature with its historical period rather than the time of writing. Hawthorne's *The Scarlet Letter,* for example, will find its setting in the colonial period.

Now, as far as the oral and written composition and other skill phases of English instruction are concerned, we may merely advance the general claim here that all such activities will be given vital content for their practice by their correlation with such social studies materials as are found in history, civics, geography, or economics. The full force of this claim will have to be realized as the detailed plans for the integration are presented, plans in which the arts of writing and speaking, the uses of reading and library skills, of grammar and spelling, are all carefully co-ordinated with the social studies content in such a way as to give vital practice in their true instrumental values. In general it may be asserted that this significant social content is a desirable substitute for the banal exercises that have been too typical of language, grammar, and composition manuals and textbooks. The direct application of the language arts to the pupil's immediate expression needs seems a more wholesome and challenging activity for high school pupils than the relation of them to formalistic exercises or the academic analysis of literary classics after the manner of university seminars.

The social content motivation of composition, both oral and written, will be illustrated in considerable detail in this chapter in such exercises as reports on current events, topical recitations, debates, group discussions, outlines, summaries, and a variety of written reports.

An illustrative plan for integration.—Inasmuch as an integration experiment, for some time to come at least, has to be fitted into a curriculum sequence in which certain well-defined blocks of subject matter in each of the courses involved are assigned or required for the semester or the year, it will be necessary to present an illustrative plan in terms of subject integration. For this purpose let us take a year's work in English and in the social studies in the senior high school, commonly described as the course in American literature and English composition, and the course in American history and civics. The plan must then fundamentally express itself in the conventional topics and activities of the two courses. Although we are aiming principally at an integration of pupil interest and experience in these two broad fields, we may, for the sake of explanation, discuss the plan in terms of correlating or integrating the content and processes of the two subjects. This integrated course may be presented in outline form as conducted by one of the writers in a year's experimentation in one of the Los Angeles high schools. The experiment was carried out with two eleventh grade classes, one of superior, and one of average, mental ability.

OUTLINE PROGRAM OF SUGGESTED PARALLEL TOPICS AND COR-
RELATED ACTIVITIES IN A YEAR'S COURSE FOR INTEGRATION IN
THE SOCIAL STUDIES AND ENGLISH IN GRADE XI OR XII

FIRST SEMESTER

SOCIAL STUDIES CONTENT

ENGLISH CONTENT AND
ACTIVITIES

I. First eight weeks

Students read through one of the standard high school textbooks in American history, for purposes of survey, orientation, and background for the year's work.

Total field of subject matter divided into eight large units, for purposes of horizontal integration with outstanding pieces of American literature:—

1. European background: discovery and exploration
2. Colonization
3. The new government
4. Democracy and westward expansion
5. Sectionalism and reunion
6. Industrial expansion
7. Internationalism
8. The United States today

I. First eight weeks

Students make self-diagnosis of achievement in reading skills and engage in daily practice for improvement in rate and comprehension in reading for remedial or constructive advancement.

Reading of some short, outstanding selection of literature typical in spirit or content in each of the periods in the history units.

II. Third, fourth, and fifth months

(Vertical correlation)

Present-day problems as suggested by current events in

II. Third, fourth, and fifth months

(Vertical correlation)

1. Free individual reading of a number of literary selec-

SOCIAL STUDIES CONTENT

ENGLISH CONTENT AND
ACTIVITIES

newspapers, radio, and other sources, especially the *historical* connections and background of these problems.

Typical problems:

1. Any outstanding event in our foreign relations

2. Any national, state, or local elections

3. The life of any person of national importance

4. Important industrial or commercial events

tions, chosen to fit into problems raised in connection with current events in social studies program

2. Narrative and explanatory oral and written expression exercises dealing with social studies problems

3. Other typical activities:

a. Technique of outlining for oral and written expression

b. How to write summary of paragraph or larger units

c. Vocabulary building and dictionary use

d. Making oral book reports

e. Improving instrumental composition technique, spelling, punctuation, pronunciation, correct grammatical usage

f. How to use index and table of contents

g. How to use library

h. Vocational exploration

i. Correlation of movements in American literature with the historical background

j. Reporting on book re-

SOCIAL STUDIES CONTENT

ENGLISH CONTENT AND
ACTIVITIES

views in newspapers
and magazines

SECOND SEMESTER

SOCIAL STUDIES CONTENT

ENGLISH CONTENT AND
ACTIVITIES

III. Sixth month

Constitutions:
National
State
Local charters
(Horizontal correlations)

III. Sixth month

Exercises, oral and written,
in explanatory and argumen-
tative types of expression,
dealing with topics in civics
or related problems in current
events.

IV. Seventh month

National government
(Horizontal correlations)

IV. Seventh month

Free reading with emphasis
on aesthetic as well as instrumental and content values.

V. Eighth month

State and local government
(Horizontal correlations)

V. Eighth, ninth, and tenth
months

Other typical English ac-
tivities:

VI. Ninth and tenth months

(Vertical correlations)

Present-day *civic* and *political* problems as suggested
by such typical current events
as:
1. Actions of Congress
2. Supreme Court decisions
3. President's messages

1. Business letter writing
2. Friendly letter writing
about local current events
3. Criticism of radio speech
4. How to take notes
5. How to write term
papers
6. How to make a bibliog-
raphy
7. Elementary methods of
research

SOCIAL STUDIES CONTENT	ENGLISH CONTENT AND ACTIVITIES
4. Federal executive and administrative acts	8. Standardized tests in English, for usage, composition, and appreciation
5. Activities of state legislature	9. Study of college entrance examinations in English and outlines of university freshman English courses
6. Events in local government	10. Social class discussions

The history and civics units.—The material for the first few weeks in the first semester in history has been divided on the large unit basis described in Chapter I. Very general descriptive captions have been given to these units, and these indicate the conventional textbook divisions, which may be described somewhat more specifically by the following outline:

Unit I. The European Background; Voyages and Expeditions of Discovery and Exploration; the Non-English Colonization Enterprises (1453 to 1763)

Unit II. The English Colonization (1607 to 1763)

Unit III. The American Revolution and the Establishment of the New Government (1763 to 1800)

Unit IV. The Development of Democracy and the Westward Movement (1800 to 1860)

Unit V. Sectionalism Due to the Slavery and Commercial Controversies; the Civil War and Reconstruction (1820 to 1876)

Unit VI. The Growth of Industrialism and National Expansion (1870 to 1914)

Unit VII. International Relations from the Monroe Doctrine Through the World War (1823 to 1918)

Unit VIII. The United States Today: the Political, Economic, and Social Problems of the Post-War Period (1918 to present)

In the second semester the general field in national, state, and local civics is indicated only in the broadest terms. It is assumed that a textbook basis will be used for the introductory survey work for this phase of the social studies for background and orientation purposes. Since the various textbooks in this field vary so greatly in general organization, more specific topics for the units are not suggested here. It will be immaterial for the purposes of correlation in what order the study of federal, state, or local government is undertaken.

Tracing the history and civics of current events.— When we enter upon the work of the third month, after the introductory survey, it is to be understood clearly that the first rapid reading of the textbook has been for background and orientation purposes only. Intensive study was not advised; it was not intended. It is now assumed that more intensive work will be undertaken *on some topics* in connection with the problems that are revealed by the study of current events. In brief, for the last three months of each semester, the method, from the point of view of social studies content, may be described as consisting of "present-day problems and their history" the first semester, and "present-day problems and their civics" the second semester.

For the moment, in this section, our explanation deals with the method of developing the subject matter of the social studies content of the course. Later sections will deal with the correlated content and activities of the English phases of the course.

The general method here proposed is to devote the major portion of the social studies content to the discussion of present-day problems, economic, social, political, international. In order to improve the student's understanding of these problems and to teach him an intelligent technique for solving them the usual method of procedure is to have the student work back from the present circumstances and situation, further and further, into the historical roots, the background and causes, the past incidents and movements that have resulted in the present culmination. The method of study will always, therefore, involve the tracing of causes from results in the historical field that has been opened up by the introductory survey and in which the pupil is prepared to orient himself as a result of the perspective reading in the early part of the semester. He is prepared now to study related paragraphs and sections in his history from the point of view of present needs. His rereading of the textbook and his expanding study of other sources of information will now be motivated by a purpose of understanding the significance of past events as related to present conditions.

It will be recognized now that the exigencies of present factors will make his intensive study of our past history a highly selective process and, necessarily, a more or less fragmentary specialization. If the study of particular present-day problems is individualized, as is also presumed in this course, the specialized intensive study will also be individualized. Some limitation on this selective specialization in intensive study will be achieved if cooperative study by small groups is undertaken of any particular contemporary problem. We must be willing, however, to defend this fragmentary special study of past events in its most extreme form, the individual specialization. The issue, frankly, is whether we are willing to justify this combination of intensive study of some elements in history and the neglect of others. The claim is just as seriously made that this method of distributed thoroughness on some topics has as much justification as a laborious distribution of superficial emphasis on all topics. This defense is based on the fact that most social studies textbooks are cluttered with an overwhelming mass of detail in deference to scholarly completeness. Some selection and evaluation is imperative if this burden of scholastic thoroughness is not to confuse the understanding and overwhelm the interest of most students. In short, it is argued that it will be more desirable for the student to know some topics thoroughly than to have a confused smattering of many topics.

It must be further argued that the method here advised will have very significant values in the way of effective study methods and a much richer promise of vital interests such as are likely to be produced by a clear understanding and a thorough knowledge of a current problem and its related information.

The method that has here been described throughout as tracing the historical antecedents of present-day problems is to be applied in a similar way the second semester in dealing with civics materials. Beginning with any current issue or question, understanding and explanations are sought, whenever necessary, by a thorough and intensive study of such topics in the structure or function of any branch of government.

Horizontal and vertical methods of integration.—In the general program for the year's work outlined above, the terms "horizontal" and "vertical" correlation are used as a suggestion of method that is expected to further the pupil's integration of interests and experiences. The terms are not intended to be taken in too strict a technical sense, but merely as a convenience for rather distinct procedures.

By horizontal correlation in the first and second month is intended a sort of chronological parallelism in topics in history and literature. For each period of history it is suggested that the student may have frequent progressive contacts with typical literary selections written during that period and reflecting the spirit or thought or characteristic experiences in the life of people at that time.

By vertical correlation we intend to imply a topical rather than a chronological relationship. For example, if a student or a class becomes interested in some current problem involved in an action of Congress and affecting foreign trade, a proper understanding of the issue may require the tracing of the history of export trade, of import trade, of related tariff regulations, of other governmental trade restrictions or encouragements. This vertical retracing through a series of steps crosses all chronological period divisions that convention or convenience may have established. Any topical or logical relationships, mainly those of effect and cause, of precedent, of background, of analogy, of contrast, of evolution and growth, may thus be traced from a present event. Loosely, the pupil's search for explanation or associations is allowed to wander as far and as long as his interest in the problem lures him, or the satisfactory solution challenges him to continue. As we shall see later, in dealing with objectives in Chapter VIII, the main purpose, *interest*—compelling, self-motivating, intrinsic interest—is being encouraged and achieved, and we are not greatly concerned into what remote fields of study it may lure. It would be no mean achievement if we could see a student now and then, from such a routine beginning, become so absorbed in a problem, that, not only for that semester, but for a whole lifetime he would be content and determined to pursue his specialized research in that field, whether the materials may be found in history, geography, civics, or economics.

Teaching remedial reading.—One of the most important phases of English work in both junior and senior high school, and one that has been too commonly neglected in the conventional courses, is the advanced instruction in reading skills. The integration of English with the social studies as suggested in the plans for this course gives exceptional opportunities to correct this failure to improve reading habits.

The neglect of instruction in the advanced reading skills is in great part a result of the confusion in the upper grade curriculum that followed the spread of the junior high school movement. In city systems where the reorganization has cut off the elementary school at the end of the sixth grade, certain elements that were formerly given considerable attention in formal courses, notably spelling, reading, and geography, were largely lost in the new curricula developed in typical junior high schools.

When the type of reading instruction formerly given in the upper grades, largely emphasizing oral expression, was dropped in the reorganized schools, it was no great loss in the child's education. Scientific research in the field of reading had demonstrated the futility of this type of instruction, if not its possibly pernicious effects on the improvement of proper habits in silent reading. It was unfortunate that when this oral type of reading was dropped, the positive findings of research were not considered as well, and a constructive program of training in the improvement of silent reading made a part of the junior high school curriculum. The work in reading was put into the English courses, and here, forgetful of the average pupil's need for improvement in reading technique, the emphasis was at once thrown in the direction of appreciative studies of the classics after the senior high school and college fashion.

It seems essential, therefore, that somehow this perfection in the instrumental improvement of reading skills must be resumed. A more sympathetic treatment of this need may be expected under the integrating program than in the isolated instruction by the specialized teacher of literature. It seems strange that teachers of English have so rarely realized their obligation to improve the reading skills of students during the secondary school period. The shortcomings of pupils in the art of silent reading will be more palpable to the teacher who sees the art inefficiently used in the instrumental applications of it in social studies subjects. Likewise, the opportunity for effective training in improvements in rate and comprehension can most conveniently be correlated with the necessities for extensive practice in the reading of materials that are not dissipated, for this objective, by incidental aesthetic values. The factual content of social studies books lends itself, perhaps better than any other materials available, for just the kind of reading experiences the students in junior and senior high school need to improve their skill in the reading art.

There are two excellent opportunities for the teacher to give this special attention to the improvement of reading in a course that combines the social studies and English as outlined in this chapter. In this discussion it is taken for granted, as research has demonstrated, that one of the most effective steps for improving the average pupil's reading ability is to urge him to increase his *rate* of reading. Only one pupil in four is an exception to the rule that quality of comprehension can be increased considerably by a simple increase in his speed of reading.

The first chance for correlating the instruction in reading with the social studies in the course here outlined is in the units of introductory survey reading during the first six or eight weeks of each semester, when students are expected to read through one of the standard textbooks in American history the first semester, in civics the second semester. The purpose of this first reading is to give a perspective of the general field and an orientation for the individual specializations in the interest centers and study projects to be pursued the rest of the time.

At the beginning of this survey reading each student should be made definitely conscious of his reading rate skill. Timed tests, for several days at the very beginning, should make it very clear to each student just what his normal rate of reading is, as well as how fast he can read if he pushes himself. Such rate tests should always be accompanied by some sort of objective test for comprehension, and it should be understood beforehand by the pupils that this check on attention and understanding will follow the rapid reading. This is partly to give the teacher a clear diagnosis of remedial reading needs, partly to show students clearly their actual ability. This should be carefully compared with such practical norms as the following: The average eight-grader should be able to read about 250 words a minute of a typical history for his grade or of the type of historical fiction often used as collateral; in the later years of the senior high school, students should be able to read their textbooks at from 300 to 350 words per minute. At either level students should be able to pass at least seventy per cent of the items in a test based on twenty or twenty-five of the outstanding facts in ten or fifteen minutes of reading. Reading rates should not be determined by one- or two-minute exercises, but for five- or ten-minute periods on several days. The labor of word counting to determine the amount read is not necessary. Accurate estimates by lines read and an average number of words per line are sufficient for practical purposes.

The weeks devoted to the introductory survey reading may be used for conscious practice by all students to increase reading rates. A weekly test and individual record charts are advised during this period to motivate efforts toward improvement. Eight weeks of such controlled practice, with daily supervised reading periods of from fifteen to thirty minutes, should result in improving nearly every student's rate from fifty to one hundred per cent, if his reading experience in the upper grades has been subjected to the typical neglect. This claim has been confirmed by a number of carefully controlled studies, and these estimates of probable improvement have been shown to be possible even for college students.

The teacher who is interested in this practical phase of instrumental English instruction should become familiar with the research studies on reading in order to aid students in intelligent self-diagnosis and remedial practice and in order to understand the specific helpfulness of such advice as "Stop vocalizing"; "Learn not to look at every word"; "Try to develop rhythmical eye-movement habits"; "Learn to read a line in four or five fixations"; "Concentrate by hurrying"; and similar concrete instructions.

The second opportunity for practice in reading skills will be found in this course in connection with the collateral or individual readings. Without neglecting the previous elements in regard to improvement of rate, a variety of specific practices for improvement of comprehension can be developed for this material. Space forbids the giving of detailed suggestions here for this type of reading instruction. The teacher must be referred again to the research literature and to the rapidly increasing volumes of advice in regard to remedial reading instruction.

Integrating advanced study skills.—The program of instruction in remedial or constructive progress in reading skills, as we pass from the standard of speed to comprehension, soon develops into a problem of teaching pupils methods of study and the use of libraries.

Much of the futility of education in the past has been due to the blind adherence of teachers to the doctrine of transfer of training—that specific practice or mental exercise would automatically and unconsciously spread or result in general improvement of the faculty exercised. Educators believed, and did not hesitate to declare their faith and to build educational programs on the theory, that, if a pupil memorized poetry or dates or foreign vocabularies, he was improving his memory; if he reasoned out mathematical problems, he was improving his reasoning powers; if he was observing phenomena, especially microscopic details, in any science laboratory, he was improving his general power of observation. Even after psychology had long discredited this conception of mental faculties and had demonstrated the dangerous fallacy of this theory of transfer in training, educators persisted in acting on this discredited faith. In the controversies that have been waged over this theory of mental discipline during the last three or four decades, two outstanding contributions by leading educational psychologists, Thorndike and Judd, have given us a far more wholesome and practical and efficient substitute for the old theory of transfer of training. Thorndike has shown, both by theoretical considerations and by impressive experimental research, that general improvements, often mistakenly thought of as transfer of training, resulting from specific study experiences, are due to the presence of identical elements. Among other such elements he includes the identity of learning or study methods in different subjects or pursuits. Judd likewise has confirmed and emphasized the effective results of what he has called "generalized experience," meaning that out of any study experience the student may consciously isolate a general idea or method which can be, equally consciously, applied to a variety of new learning situations. We may combine the two theories and, by using what may perhaps be recognized as a more clarifying descriptive term, say that out of any study experience a student may consciously recognize a "concept of method," and that, when this method has been clearly and consciously understood as such, that technique of learning or study may be applied to any other suitable situation.

We may reasonably conclude, then, that one of the most helpful, practical, permanent results of instruction in any subject would be such concepts of methods of study. Education thus, instead of a blind belief in automatic, unconscious transfers or improvements, would undertake as one of its chief objectives the training in a variety of study methods. Students, especially in the secondary schools and college, would and should be equipped with a whole arsenal of study methods, a variety of weapons or tools, each fitted, by a conscious understanding of their purposes and possibilities, to the most efficient learning of any new material or the solution of any new intellectual problem.

Out of the supervised study movement and out of the diagnostic technique of the standardized testing movement, many of the most important concepts of method, specific study techniques, have been identified, and training in their efficient use has come to be included in the educational ideals of many of the best-informed and progressive teachers and curriculum makers.

The responsibility for a large share in this conscious instruction of students in how to study, in intelligent adjustment and application of a variety of techniques to the demands of different materials and purposes, is the privilege which we are claiming especially for the teachers of social studies and English in the high schools. We therefore urge this as a specially important part in the program of the teacher who is assuming the responsibility for both subjects in an integrating course. One of the advantages in the combined course, indeed, lies in the fact that the various important identified methods of study need not be allocated to the two departments to avoid duplications or important omissions. Details of these phases of integrating the work of English and social studies, in the teaching of study methods and library use, have been presented in Chapter V.

The place of grammar instruction.—Teachers who have the specialized English instructor's point of view will be likely to ask what place is given, if any, to the instruction in grammar in the integrated course. Frankly, an extremely negative attitude is taken, which may be summarized in two definite statements: (1) No provision is made for instruction in formal grammar; (2) any attention given to questions of grammatical usage is incidental to occasional drills in correct oral expression and to individual needs revealed in written compositions.

It is assumed that, if the curriculum is to require instruction in formal grammar in either the junior or senior high school course in English, the semester of technical grammar should be taught in some other year. If all instruction in the social studies and English for the six years of secondary school should follow the integrating method, what is to become of a technical or formal English grammar course is too hypothetical and remote to demand an answer here. A suggestion may be ventured, however, that that formal part of English should probably be integrated with the introductory courses in foreign language, the place where it has its most practical and vital application.

The aesthetic element in literature.—One of the important elements that must not be neglected by the teacher who is attempting integration in the social studies and English fields is the appreciation of aesthetic elements in the literature that is used in the combined course.

English teaching as a specialty may be said to include

three distinct values in the materials and activities that have become characteristic of instruction in that subject. These may briefly be designated as the instrumental, the aesthetic, and the content values. By the instrumental we mean those activities that are involved in the correct and effective language usage in conversation and oral and written composition. By the aesthetic we mean those values, both of form and content, that are especially involved in the emotional reactions and appreciations of literary beauty. In the content values we have specially in mind the intellectual, informational elements found in a piece of literature or the factual, non-aesthetic elements in a pupil's compositions. The teaching of English has largely become a professional specialty in both college and secondary schools by the identification and emphasis placed on the first and second of these elements, the instrumental and the aesthetic. The two, in the common practice of English teachers, have often been combined so as to emphasize the reciprocal relations of composition activities and the aesthetic factors of literary studies. This combination was a natural one and yet it has been carried to such an extreme that in composition instruction the instrumental has been subordinated to the aesthetic to such a degree as to obscure or destroy the practical uses of the pupil's expression exercises.

Even where a reasonable distinction and balance is maintained between the instrumental and the aesthetic factors, by the better teachers, it is not uncommon to find a lack of attention on the social content, the thought, of a classic, because of the efforts to induce an appreciation of such form elements as rhyme, rhythm, meter, diction, style, literary forms and types. It is the emphasis on these formal elements, which are really only adapted to the literary appreciation or criticism of the cultured adult, that has really distinguished the teaching of English, first in the colleges, and later in the high schools, as a specialized subject. This formal aesthetic element, inducing the critical analysis of classics, since it has gone to the training of the connoisseur of literature, is naturally the ultimate objective of all literary study and instruction. The equally natural overemphasis on this aesthetic appreciation of formal elements in the teaching of the immature, in preference to, and often to the neglect of, the thought content, has much to do with the failure of a great deal of English teaching in the secondary schools. Because of youth's immaturity, the instruction has often been suspected by students of an insincere affectation of tastes on the teacher's part and has produced a revulsion of disinterest and dislike instead of the interested appreciation that was intended. When the English teacher, then, becomes a subject-minded specialist, there is the serious danger that this devotion to the aesthetic may result in an esoteric arrogance.

Now when the teacher who has not achieved that ultra attitude of subject-mindedness, and whose educational aims are still child-centered, attempts integration by introducing literary readings and expression exercises into a social studies background, there is a corresponding danger of giving offense by an unbalanced disregard of the aesthetic in both reading and composition. Again we have the teacher making a natural mistake. The more wholesome use of literature for its content values, and of composition for its instrumental uses, may easily result in a neglect of worth-while appreciations which should be encouraged to some degree, because experiences of this sort are as significant in the adolescent's needs for present interests and permanent tastes as the informational or auxiliary factors in reading, speaking, and writing.

The teacher who has assumed the responsibility of integrating a pupil's aesthetic experiences with his quest for social information, thinking, and expression may reasonably hope to achieve much of the appreciation results by a procedure of wholesome contagion, by a courageous policy of superficial disregard of the literary critical technique. If one has a genuine faith in the artistic excellence and appeal of a classic and a true understanding of the aesthetic susceptibility of human nature, he has a right to trust for effective natural results from the contagion of readings that are motivated by interests and values of content, or by the needs for effective expression. Even such a program of superficial contact will be more like the typical adult's perusal of literature than the artificial technique of the specialist in English who has adopted his methods of higher and lower criticism, his parsing and scanning, his analysis of structure and style, from the erudite scholasticism of the Latin, Greek, and Hebrew grammarians and professors.

Adjustments to traditional practices and points of view, however, may involve too delicate a situation to make such a natural program for literary study quite adequate. A critical compromise may, therefore, be advisable in the integrating program. Standard appreciation techniques of the specialists should be critically examined, and humanized adaptations to the secondary school students' abilities and needs should be attempted to make the program seem reasonably adequate in its emphasis on aesthetic elements in all literature that is used as a means of developing socialized interests and understanding.

An interesting movement in the field of English teaching is the recent reformation along these lines attempted by many of the most thoughtful teachers of this subject. This movement has usually been referred to as the "free reading" program, and advocates a freer choice and a more superficial contact with a number of books instead of the painful "frazzling" of one or two classics for a semester's work. There has always been this progressive element prominent in the "English Round Table" leaders who for two or three decades have rebelled against the dictation as to what and how they should teach as laid down in the College Entrance Requirements in English. This progressive element must be given credit for a long and consistent struggle against the stultifying influence of this college dictation. As a matter of fact, the secondary school teachers of English must be given credit for having been more persistent and more successful than any other single professional group in their revolt against this university strangling of the high school's greater service to its students and to the community.

Free reading of selected literature.—This topic might easily be challenged as involving a contradiction or a paradox. The movement for free, natural reading has come to be recognized widely as more likely to arouse interests and build good taste in literary selection than the elaborate class exercises in appreciation.

In some of the free-reading experiments, freedom has been interpreted to mean that for his English literature classes any pupil might read any book he chose and make some sort of informal report on it in class or to the teacher personally. It was hoped and believed that such reading, because of its freedom, would stimulate interest, and that, in connection with the pupil's report or the discussion of the book, the teacher would have a chance to raise and correct standards of taste in selection and appreciation. This was done, when it was done, by contrasting the banal and unworthy with the better books. Frank criticisms, honest recommendations, and sincere contagions were relied on to improve tastes in reading—it was all a natural real-life activity and, with the clever, enthusiastic, and sympathetic teacher, became as effective an influence for good reading as the recommendations of one adult may become for another.

The freedom in reading was, however, seriously abused in many instances. Juveniles, thrillers, and the least desirable of popular books, or specialized reading in some field that had no merit toward building aesthetic standards in literature, were often permitted in English courses, and little effort was made to modify, redirect, or elevate children's standards. Even this type of activity, with little worthy result on the formation of good taste, might be defended in contrast to the type of scholastic literary study that bred disinterest and dislike for the classics. In addition to avoiding this serious negative result, it might fairly be claimed that students were at least encouraged to read, to form the habit of reading, and to recognize the possibilities of reading as an interesting leisure activity. Perhaps the inculcating of this habit and this attitude toward reading is a more reasonable objective, at least for the pre-adolescents of the junior high school period, than the artificial forcing of literary tastes into the most cultured adult molds.

The topic chosen for this section, and the procedure that is implied, may therefore easily be recognized as a reasonable compromise rather than a contradiction. It implies that the free choices in reading, by each pupil, shall be prescribed within a range somewhat limited by teacher selection. The range may be wide, generously wide, and the selection may be individual, but the school shall not sanction the banal juveniles and worthless thrillers as a part of school work. These will be read on the responsibility of the child and the home, never with the encouragement or approval of the teacher. After the initial selection of a list of acceptable books by the teacher, the pupil may be left free to make his choice. It is assumed, if the ideal procedure may be advised, that all books in such a list shall be readily available to the students in either the school or a special room library, preferably in the room. It is also advised, as a matter of good teaching, that the teacher shall, as far as time permits, discuss the individual reading selections with each pupil, advising, consulting interests and preferences, urging variety, but never dictating or requiring. If a student selects a book, and after some sampling, wishes to drop it and try another, he should be given the adult's privilege, though his abandonment may be made a matter of frank discussion and encouraging advice, if there is any evidence of unreasonable whim. The direction of interests in many cases is to be adjusted with tact, sympathy, and sincerity, never in the spirit of compulsion or authority.

Some criticisms of integration.—Now that we have the general plan of integration before us, as exemplified in the extreme correlation of the social studies and English, but capable of a number of other subject combinations, it may be well to consider some of the difficulties that are commonly raised by teachers, especially if their co-operation in such an integrating enterprise is required by a curriculum department or other administrative agency.

One of the first objections that is often raised by teachers who are doubtful about the feasibility of combining the work in two or more subjects is, "How do you cover the required ground?" If subject requirements for a semester or a year are expressed in customary terms of fixed quantities of subject matter, it must be admitted that the difficulty is often a serious one. The question is often answered, however, by agreeing that the teacher may have considerable leeway and may use his own discretion about omissions and special emphasis. The fundamental philosophy of integration, with its point of view centered on pupil needs and interests, makes such a generous concession imperative to the success of the plan.

The question should be frankly answered, "You do not have to cover a prescribed field of subject matter in the same balanced, systematic, logical completeness." Strict traditional requirement would contradict the essential spirit of the integrating enterprise. A courageous disregard of many factual details if they are not demanded by the needs of individual pupils' problems, an unbalanced use of subject elements, with learning emphasis by some students and neglect by others, must be recognized as inevitable accompaniments of the plan.

If a compromise on conventional requirements, in the form of administrative tests on fundamentals, is necessary, definite time allotments can be set aside for drill periods on such elements. The use of workbooks and study guide lesson sheets, prepared by the teacher to meet the supervisory surveys, is advised as the best means of complying with these demands and as resulting in the least interference with the general integration plans. Such work sheets can be highly individualized both in their diagnosis of pupil needs and in the learning practice necessary to meet the tests for mastery of fundamentals.

Objections of English teachers.—Some of the sharpest attacks on integration have come from teachers of English who charge that the social studies are trying to swallow the work in English. This danger of the subordination of the one department to the other must be admitted to be real. The integration plan is only a part of a larger movement, the growing recognition of the importance of training for civic and social efficiency in the secondary schools. This movement will not be denied. Popular demand and social leadership are back of the educational administrators in the movement to increase the time to be given all phases of social studies work in the public schools. One of the most certain points of invasion for this movement is in the department of English. Teachers of that subject can do several things to meet the difficulty in which they are sure to find themselves in an increasing degree in the near future. They may shortsightedly resist in the spirit of subject-minded defenders of their specialty. This will be a personal, bread-and-butter defense, natural enough, but certain to be ineffective. They may re-examine critically their objectives and see how, by revision, they can better adapt their work to the instrumental and practical needs of students, and to a more direct contribution to social values. In fact, the subject of English must, in the near future, be able to vindicate itself clearly as one of the social studies, or be integrated with them or subordinated to them and lose its standing as an independent department.

Special teaching qualities needed.—When a teacher of average ability hears some of the ambitious integration plans expounded by one who has the enthusiasm of the pioneer and the courage of the experimenter, there is likely to be the response of modest mediocrity, "Such a plan requires a super-teacher; it isn't feasible for most of us." This confession of limitations and this fear of failure with an ambitious new enterprise have some basis for consideration. Not every teacher can hope to carry out an integration plan successfully. A super-teacher may not be needed, but special qualities are necessary, special demands for self-development must be met, and adjustment to experimental situations must be made. Success in an integration plan cannot be expected for a strictly subject-minded teacher, one who has devoted years, not only to the experience of teaching one subject, but one who has during all that time specialized all cultural and study efforts to that single field. The teacher who has not had a broad-minded outlook in his own culture, the English teacher who has no interests in history reading, or the social studies teacher who is not in sympathetic touch with much of the best literature can only hope to get along with an integration program, if he is willing to undertake a serious revolution in his own study habits. It seems a serious reflection on our university courses when we find teachers helpless with the consciousness of such narrow specializations in their preparation and interests; but we have to recognize the fact, and admit its validity as a serious obstacle for success in the present progressive movement with its child-centered point of view.

In addition to this broader cultural demand on the teacher, we also have to recognize certain other professional attitudes which are essential for success with the newer methods. A teacher who cannot resist the temptation to a striving for new and showy effects, one who cannot reconcile the possibility of development in intangibles at the sacrifice of mastery of fundamentals, one who fears his ability to keep a balanced control between play and study, one who cannot withstand the demands of pupils for the old and familiar types of study tasks—one, in short, who is too ready to admit that "fusion will become confusion"—such a teacher should probably hesitate or refuse to undertake such a serious departure from routine technique as the integration program involves.

Extreme forms of integration and fusion.—Another difficulty in planning an integration program lies in the lack of agreement among its advocates as to a basic definition and description of the plan. This difficulty has already been hinted at in the introductory sections, where provisional explanations were given as a working basis for discussion. The distinction between subject correlation and the more extreme pupil-centered integration must now be made more precise. The difference in definitions hinges on whether one's point of view is expressed in terms of objectives only or, on the other hand, of method and materials. The latter point of view has been taken in our discussion so far; we may now compare and contrast with this the definition and description of integration from the angle of objectives. Integration, so considered, is not something the teacher does, but something the student does; it is not to be defined in terms of teaching method, but as a learning activity.

In a *Social Studies Leaflet,* the official organ of the Southern California Social Science Association, one of the curriculum directors of the Los Angeles schools, where various progressive plans have been experimented with for several years under official supervision, we find the following clear-cut distinction between correlation and integration:

> *Correlation* is a process of arranging the content of related fields in such a manner that each of the fields is mutually contributory to the other. . . . This entire mass may be considered as one entity and may be taught either by one teacher having sufficient grasp of the fields of learning or by teachers from each of the several fields in close co-operation.

> *Integration* is the psychological process by which an individual, actuated by a real desire or vital interest, brings to bear upon a life situation knowledge, skills, habits, and attitudes from all pertinent fields of learning, using the emotional and mental resources of his entire personality, which in turn is more or less permanently changed in its entirety.

> *Integration* is essentially a psychological phenomenon, while *correlation* is a pedagogical manipulation of subject matter. Through popular usage, integration is being taken to connote outstanding examples of correlation. However, in their true meaning, the difference is not one of *degree,* but one of *kind.* Cor-

relation is a means, integration is an end. Correlation may be done by the teacher in his arrangement of teaching materials; integration must be done by the pupil in using his collective learning for a definite *purpose*. Reselection and rearrangement of subject matter usually need to go much further than simple correlation before genuine integration can be achieved.

If we recognize the relation between objectives on the one hand and materials and methods on the other, there need be no confusion or controversy about the definitions of integration and correlation. If we choose to reserve the term integration for the learner's mental activities and experiences, we may describe the teacher's method as a deliberate planning, a correlation of materials and activities, no matter how desirable it may seem to disguise the guidance from the student or to minimize it in our technical definition of integration. It is merely a question of the extent to which an intelligent and sympathetic teacher can go in the guidance of student thinking by means of class plans and individual direction. In some of the progressive discussions, it must be admitted, there is some overenthusiastic juggling with an esoteric vocabulary of "pedagoose," lately reinforced by some of the extravagances of a Gestalt psychology, which have produced confusion rather than conviction in the minds of some teachers who were trying to understand the real significance of the integration plan. Such verbal juggling has too often been accompanied by a spirit of arrogant impatience instead of a willingness to meet the challenge for clearness and definiteness in explaining the new plans. As a natural reaction, the suspicions and charges of vagueness and planlessness have been aroused against integration. These defects are not inherent in the plan, but in some of the excesses of enthusiastic advocates.

Integration with life.—One of the motives that impels the enthusiasts of all types of progressive education, but especially those who are trying to build up a new philosophy for the teacher by the integrating program, is the substitution of realities for the artificial system of academic tasks that have made learning a routine in subject matter too often lacking in interest and vitality from the standpoint of youth. The reality for which they plead is the natural, real-life need. It is a development of Dewey's dictum that "Education is not a preparation for life, it is life"; it is the stimulating and satisfying of present felt needs, not the cramming for hypothetical adult needs; not a memorizing of knowledge, facts, information, but a growth in skills and attitudes by the immediate use of any knowledge that may be necessary, regardless of its subject relations.

It is now evident why some advocate integration in the form of this extreme disregard of all traditional, logical subject boundaries. The student's integrating process involves a consciousness of purposefulness in all his reading and study, a relation of learning to problems that have the clear-cut compulsion of real-life values. The student of junior or senior high school age, of average or higher mental ability, is mature enough to recognize realities in vocational, civic, social, and ethical problems that can vitalize all possible efforts in study and expression in the social sciences. It is just because he is recognizing these realities as the criteria of imposed academic subjects and tasks that he finds so much in the conventional school work to condemn and resist. The effort of progressive education to meet these natural criteria of youth intelligently and the teacher's willingness to let the student's own needs and interests determine his mental activities constitute the program of integrating learning with life. It is the labor of setting the stage for such purposeful activity in thinking and learning that defines the teacher's place in integration, and also defines the process from the child-centered point of view.

Vocational exploration, judgments and ambitions about standards of living, ideals about companionship, friendships, and recreational activities, tastes in reading and amusements, consciousness of civic and community obligations—all these criteria are vivid and vital enough in secondary school days to provide interests and arouse problems to impose realistic demands upon history, literature, current reading, movies, and the radio. These interests and problems will be the present realities of the life of youth, not the imposed possibilities of adulthood. Facts as such, no matter how systematically the logic of experience may have grouped them, have no sanctity because of such traditional grouping, if in this conventional subject setting they do not contribute to the student's own objectives, standards, and attitudes. The student has a right to demand those learning activities and materials that contribute clearly to the understanding and orientation of his own present-day life. It is this that integration advocates have in mind when they dwell on the exact interpretation of the term in the sense of its essential derivation. This is back of their insistence that "the whole is more than the sum of all its parts." The student's integration of the subject parts, the elements of the teacher's correlation, produces an individual, personal product which is not merely a simple process of addition of fractions with a common denominator. It is an appropriation and an application of the whole result to his understanding of life.

BIBLIOGRAPHY

Chubb, Percival: *Teaching of English in the Elementary and Secondary School.* (Revised and enlarged edition.) New York: The Macmillan Company, 1929.

Crawford, C. C., and McDonald, L. P.: *Modern Methods in Teaching Geography*. Boston: Houghton Mifflin Company, 1929, Chapter VI.

Gray, W. S., and Whipple, G.: *Improving Instruction in Reading*. Chicago: University of Chicago Press, 1933.

Hopkins, Thomas, and Armentrout, W. D.: *Principles of Integration*. In Department of Superintendence, National Education Association, Ninth Yearbook. Department of Superintendence, 1931.

Johnson, Henry: *The Teaching of History in Elementary and Secondary Schools*. New York: The Macmillan Company, 1920, Chapter XV.

Knowlton, Daniel C.: *History and the Other Social Studies in the Junior High School*. New York: Charles Scribner's Sons, 1926, Chapters I, VIII.

Logassa, H.: *Historical Fiction and Other Reading References for History Classes in Junior and Senior High Schools*. Philadelphia: McKinley Publishing Company, 1934.

Pitkin, Walter: *The Art of Reading*. New York: McGraw-Hill Book Company, 1931.

Sweeney, F. G., Barry, E. F., and Schoelkopf, A. E.: *Western Youth Meets Eastern Culture*. New York: Bureau of Publications, Teachers College, Columbia University, 1932.

Wilson, H. E.: *The Fusion of Social Studies in Junior High Schools*. Cambridge: Harvard University Press, 1933.

PERIODICALS

Rugg, Harold O.: "A Preface to the Reconstruction of the American School Curriculum." *Teachers' College Record*, March, 1926, pp. 600-616.

Werner, R. C.: "Music and Pictures." *Historical Outlook*, November, 1927, pp. 330-331.

CHAPTER VII

MODIFYING TRADITIONAL METHODS

The relation of old and new methods.—The progressive methods that have been outlined in the preceding chapters may reasonably be considered as experiments that have been on trial for several years by pioneer teachers in different parts of the country. Most of them have been undertaken in cities or sections where teaching methods have been strongly influenced by experimental schools or by curriculum departments or by the example and enthusiasm of enterprising teachers who have been thoughtfully disturbed by the meagre results of traditional routine in teaching and have had the courage and ingenuity to modify their classroom procedure. Most of these pioneers have been strongly affected by two distinct influences: the new philosophy of education largely developed by John Dewey and his followers, and the findings of important research studies made by education departments in some of the leading universities. The methods that have been described and advocated for the improvement of instruction in the social sciences are a part of a larger movement that is affecting every subject and every level of our educational system.

It must not be assumed, however, that these progressive movements, so active in advocating a thorough reconsideration of the public school curriculum in all departments and a change of purposes and methods in all our teaching, necessarily involve a complete abandonment of all the materials and methods of the past. A few radicals have, in their enthusiasm, gone to that extreme. It is one of the natural prerogatives of a reformer to be an extremist. Excessive denunciations of previous or present orthodox practices by zealots and innovators are unfortunate, for, when they impinge on the resistance of the conservative, they prejudice the cause of progress and rouse antagonism to the spirit of the reformer without getting a thoughtful consideration of his new ideas. It has been our purpose throughout the discussion of these progressive plans to explain them in such a way as to emphasize their practical and educational values without involving any of the unnecessary excesses of theorists and enthusiasts. We have tried to maintain this critical and analytical spirit toward the progressive schemes, without condemnation of conventional practices, because we believed the values could thus be made clearer and more acceptable than if we had employed an esoteric manner and a theoretical superiority with reference to the traditional methods.

It remains, in the present chapter, to undertake a critically constructive examination of some of the methods and materials in common use in the social studies for the purpose of conserving some of the best elements in that practice, either just as they are or by some sensible modifications that the progressive experiments have shown to be necessary for a more successful program of education.

The place of the textbook in the new plans.—In connection with the description of the new methods frequent reference has been made to the use of textbooks. Some of the references may provoke a critical disapproval from the more extreme advocates of the new plans, some of which have basically been conceived as protests against textbook teaching. In considering the values and uses of the textbook here, there is no intention to defend textbook teaching as such. The traditional slavish use of a textbook for purposes of daily assignments and oral recitation has merited the criticisms that have been heaped upon it by progressive teachers and supervisors. The deadening effects of oral question-and-answer testing on minute details of short daily assignments, especially in the factual content of the social studies, are fully recognized and admitted.

While the protest against this mechanical grind over a logical condensation of subject matter is urged as the most wholesome element in all the new methods, the complete rejection of the textbook is considered an unwise extreme, which will make it difficult, if not impossible, for most teachers to make even an experimental beginning with any of the progressive plans. This may be partly the fault of teaching habit and conservative prejudice, but it is also a reasonable recognition of real educational values in the typical textbook. The time is already at hand when new types of school books, better adapted to the progressive plans, are beginning to supplant the specialist's cyclopedic compendiums. Even these books must retain many of the efficient helps and features of organization, selection, grading, style, and form that have been developed as pedagogic arts by authors and publishers. The textbook, even in its present unrevised form, has such significant values for the unit plan, for parallel use with workbooks, as a basic reference manual for a present-day problem course, for socialized or laboratory plans, and for integrating courses that it cannot be abandoned because it has been abused. The textbook in all the social sciences is still the most convenient and best-organized condensed summary of available fundamental information. It is still the one most useful book for giving an introductory survey for perspective on any topic or unit in history, geography, or civics. Textbooks may have the disadvantage of excessive detail, but, in general, they are still the best adaptations in vocabulary and style that we have for the immature. This may not be altogether true in the social studies; notable efforts to popularize these subjects by such writers as H. G. Wells, Hendrik Van Loon, and V. M. Hillyer cannot be ignored. Yet we cannot overlook the distortions of special pleading for an economic theory in Wells' *Outline of History* or the cynical flippancies of Van Loon as serious drawbacks to the use of their books for basic reading in schools. Further, while we may agree that the logical arrangement and completeness of subject matter is not always the best psychological arrangement for progressive teaching purposes, there is no serious drawback in having students have some contact with such logical arrangements in their general reading in a course. Different textbooks in any field still present the most convenient means for bringing students in contact with compact accounts from different points of view or with different degrees of difficulty. They are still the most convenient sources as basic reference books for the fields they cover, especially in a simplified and condensed form suited to the practical needs of younger readers.

Both the necessity and the limitations of the textbook are recognized in the Report of the American Historical Association's Commission on the Social Studies.[1] The Commission declares that the textbook "will doubtless play an important rôle in social science instruction for many years," but it advises that the teacher supplement the textbook "by an abundance of collateral reading, by books, newspapers, and magazines, by maps, photographs, charts, models, motion pictures, museums, and materials for constructive activities, and by carefully organized journeys, excursions, and field studies in the home community and, if possible, in more distant regions."

The supplementing will not be confined to collateral

[1] In *Conclusions and Recommendations*, p. 79.

reading, but should include all sorts of graphic and illustrative materials and realia, and the study activities should be accompanied and enforced by construction projects and excursions.

One of the important innovations that is suggested for a textbook course in the social studies is the use of a variety of parallel textbooks instead of the exclusive use of a single basic text by all students. This is in no sense intended as a recommendation that parallel texts be used as the chief source of collateral reading. The method advised may be readily illustrated by a unit-plan course largely based on a traditional logical outline, which may be conceived as the first, and easiest, step in the direction of progressive experimentation. In such a course it is advised that the original perspective reading should be so planned that eight or ten different texts are used instead of one. At the end of each unit the books are shifted around so that each student gets the experience of doing his basic reading in a different text for each of the units. This plan will be found available in any school where there are sufficient numbers of duplicate copies in the library to supply all members of the class, a condition that will be found in many schools. The consent and cooperation of the librarian to have such sets of textbooks issued to a teacher for a room library for the semester should not be difficult to obtain.

The purpose of this plan is to give each student a variety of contacts; to give the class as a whole different points of view for each unit; to secure a student reaction as to the relative merits of various authors in matters of clearness, interest, style; to provide a composite of several accounts and an insight into comparative evaluations of successive periods, movements, topics, and facts by different authors. If this method is employed, it will also have a wholesome effect on the teacher's evaluation of materials for unit tests, if these are conscientiously and fairly made. Such tests should include only elements common to all the texts used. Moreover, these common elements will give the teacher an interesting, comparative perspective as to details that are considered essential or unimportant by different experts in the field.

In such a plan it is suggested that some regard be given to the varying degrees of difficulty of textbooks intended for successive school levels. In a junior high school class most of the books will be those written for that level, but a few senior high school texts in the same subject may be included, to be tried out by the brighter pupils. In a senior high school class several college textbooks may be introduced in the same way.

Modifying the recitation.—It will be helpful for the improvement of teaching if we cease to think of the class period as a recitation. This term is an unfortunate legacy of the old ungraded rural school days when one teacher was confronted with a miscellaneous collection of pupils from beginners to at least eighth-graders. The teacher's daily schedule had to provide for five- or ten-minute testing periods for each group of two or three in every subject and at every level. With the small number of pupils in a class and with the short time available for each, the testing by oral question and answer was a natural method and quite efficient, since it left each child the greater part of the day for study in preparation.

With the introduction of the graded school, and still more with the development into departmentalized instruction at the secondary level, this use of the period when a teacher met a class in the same type of oral recitation testing grew into one of the most inane and inefficient practices any system of education has ever developed. With most of the pupil's day taken up with class periods, and with most of the time consumed in this ineffective oral testing, there was little time left to the child for effective study. The school day became a boresome succession of classes in which all had to spend most of each period listening to the teacher's efforts to probe the lack of preparation in others. The accompanying evils of expecting home preparation for these futile testing recitations grew to proportions which have roused the condemnation of parents, and, in a few cases, the official disapproval of administrators.

If the oral recitation habit is abandoned during the class period, and the hour is transformed into one predominantly given to learning instead of testing, there are several incidental problems of method that must be given some consideration. Natural procedures to substitute will be the silent, individual, supervised study and the oral, co-operative discussion period, both already explained. In connection with the study discussions we find the question-and-answer technique almost as prominent as in the recitation, but motivated in quite a different spirit and expressed in a different form. The modifications of the question-and-answer method, therefore, deserve some further explanation to direct them toward the more progressive ideals of instruction.

Improving question-and-answer methods.—The predominating purpose of the teacher in the use of this method is likely to be betrayed by the kind of questions asked. In the formal recitation-testing program, questions are likely to be of the factual, informational type. In the co-operative study discussion period, questions requiring thought and explanation, especially questions of the "why" or "how" type, will be prominent. The factual recitation questioning is the sort of exercise that any teacher with a little experience can go through offhand without particular preparation. Thought questions, on the other hand, must usually be prepared carefully in advance. One of the modifications urged in adapting the old technique to new uses is the provision of a set of problem questions for class thinking and discussion for each lesson or for chapter units.

In connection with the use of the question-and-answer method a number of specific suggestions seem advisable:

1. Rarely give a question dealing with less than a paragraph unit. This will encourage more extended expression from the student. Occasional exceptions are involved when secondary questions arise out of pupil responses or the class discussion.

2. Avoid specific fact questions about dates, numbers, names, places. This is merely suggested as a technical device to keep away from the recitation-testing spirit in questioning. It does not imply that such data are to be ignored altogether in the student's learning.

3. Always address questions to the whole class, not to some individual student. This standard technique is merely mentioned in the promotion of general interest of all members of the class to all questions.

4. Try to avoid, as much as possible, any system in calling on pupils to respond to questions. Distribution of questions to all members of the class must be made in such a way as to make it practically impossible for students to compute their "turn to answer." All must be kept thinking about all suggestions made.

5. The question-and-answer method is not adapted to reports on collateral material. Whether the questioning has the testing or the explanatory purpose, it should largely be confined to the materials covered in the text.

6. Do not insist on formality in the pupils' response. Allow pupils to remain seated, largely to save time. This informality of the discussion period is contrasted with the more formal exercise when the student comes before the class for a topical report.

7. Plan deliberately to transform the discussion period into an informal group conversation, with a generous contribution of questions, suggestions, and comments from the class members without the formality of being called on if the general spirit of courteous consideration of others is properly observed.

Discussion with open textbooks.—The foregoing explanation of the question-and-answer method has intimated the desirability of using part of the class period occasionally in discussions with open textbooks. Some further practical suggestions may be made for such discussion periods:

1. Such discussions with open textbooks are especially advised for detailed explanation of advance assignments, for unit orientations, or for the introduction of problems.

2. Selected sections of assignments may be read aloud or silently in class, with the teacher raising questions or explaining difficult or important elements. This procedure, however, should not be allowed to deteriorate into a typical elementary school oral reading class.

3. In connection with these textbook discussion periods teachers should plan occasional exercises for the purpose of teaching students how to outline. The main purpose here is to help students see the importance of the co-ordination of a few important ideas and the relation of subordinate items to main divisions. Such outlining should probably never be car-

ried in high school to a finer detail than the identification of the three or four main divisions of a chapter or large section and one degree of subordinate topics.

4. During the discussion period the class may deal with word studies based on the textbook. For each chapter the teacher should prepare lists of distinctive words having specific values as important ideas, usually technical, in history and civics. To this list should be added, for word study, all proper names of any importance. Both pronunciation and meaning of all terms should be taught. Some of the specially significant technical terms should be frequently reviewed. Distinctive word study tests, especially of the matching type, should be prepared to emphasize this phase of the work. One of the most important permanent results of the high school history course should be a thorough understanding of practically all such terms. These lists may be based on such research studies as the Pressey Lists.

5. The open textbook discussion period should also be used to explain or to test the pupils' understanding of all maps, pictures, and graphs given in the text. The attention and understanding of all such illustrative material is usually neglected by being taken for granted.

6. Use the discussion period, especially in connection with advance assignments, for giving the students bird's-eye view explanations and for bringing out the relationships of the new units to those preceding and to those that involve important present-day problem values.

7. Discussion periods may, in the case of some individual students, be made the basis for correlation with necessary remedial reading work. The history

teacher who uses the reading assignment in connection with class discussions will be in a position to discover deficiencies of students, especially in comprehension.

8. In connection with the word studies pupils should be taught the independent use of the dictionary, encyclopedia, and textbook index, and the relation of these helps to one another. Such references for new or difficult words will not only give the meaning, but also the events in connection with which the term has its origin, setting, or use.

9. In connection with the outlining and with the bird's-eye view explanation, the teacher should use the discussion period, especially by the forward and backward use of the textbook, for the purpose of making students conscious of the sequence of events and of the author's logic in the development and explanation of topics and movements.

10. The discussion period may also be used as a basis for guiding the students' independent study of advance assignments by evaluating the topics. Important events that are to be emphasized should be pointed out, and in some cases less important sections should also be indicated as such.

New motive in topical recitations.—The topical recitation was probably the earliest innovation introduced by teachers in recognition of the inefficiency of the old recitation method. As the name indicates, however, some of the spirit and intent of the recitation, that is, oral pupil testing, was retained. In connection with most of the new plans we have discussed the topical recitation as a device has been referred to several times, and the name, because of its common use, has been retained because of its descriptive implications. It should now be made plain that the form and even the name have been retained for convenience only, with no intention to suggest that an oral report by a pupil should be made for the purpose of testing or grading him on his reading or study, at least not primarily. It may incidentally have that value, but the fundamental spirit of such oral reports should be far different, and should be so understood by the pupils. Oral reports should serve a two-fold purpose: (1) to bring information, individually gathered, to all other members of the class; and (2) to give the student an opportunity for practice in one of the most valuable expression skills he can acquire in school.

Notebooks and outlining.—Among the comparatively recent methods that have come into common use in social studies classrooms as a substitute for the oral recitation is the compilation of notebooks based on a semester's course. Certain fixed types of work have become characteristic in this notebook making activity. Some are devoted to daily mechanical outlining of the textbook assignments or to the recording of phrases or sentences that supply the answers to a series of questions written on the blackboard or that are given at the end of a textbook chapter. Some are given to topical summaries in the form of paragraph compositions or longer themes—a variety of written topical recitation, based either on the student's textbook study or on assigned topics in collateral reading. Variations of this type result in a collection of freer compositions on social studies topics, similar to the student's English theme book. A more recent common practice is to make the history, civics, or geography notebook a specialized scrapbook containing a collection of pictures cut from newspapers or magazines, with comments ranging from mere titles to rather extended composition.

In too many cases this notebook work has become a futile sort of busywork. The origin of the device can probably be traced to a very imperfect understanding on the teacher's part of two marked educational movements, the spread of supervised study as a substitute for the recitation, and the application of construction activities to give a realistic motivation to some of the school subjects. The notebook, especially in some of the more elaborate products with original artistic bindings and cleverly designed titles and arrangements, made impressive concrete showpieces to advertise the work of the pupils to parents and principals. This temptation to achieve showy results and the misunderstanding of educative activity as any sort of definite construction work have thrown the whole device of notebook making into disrepute with thoughtful teachers. Pupils, however, have usually shown a very definite approval of the method. The activity was to them more interesting than the recitation; it freed them from the teacher's minute and random probing for memorized facts; and the notebook transformed the indefinite study of a book into a more concrete and specific task analogous to the assignments in mathematics. The charm of the mechanical and routine completion of an assignment had its lure in making the method popular.

In pointing out the defects resulting from a short-sighted use of the notebook method, the modifications necessary to justify its use in an educative program have been broadly implied. Thoughtful outlining deserves some practice in the social studies courses. Questions that compel a reorganized expression of textbook language and some study of relationships, free composition that involves an understanding of new problems, and similar materials that challenge thought and require originality of expression, all show the possibilities of notebook work. With such avoidance of purely mechanical activity, the teacher can adapt the device to progressive methods as well as to the more conventional program.

Adapting the lecture method to high school use.—The

imitation of formal university lecturing in social science
classes has been carried to unreasonable extremes in
junior and senior high schools, especially by younger
teachers of these subjects who have only recently escaped
from some inspiring major professor. The imitation is
both a compliment to the model and a betrayal of inadequate training in teaching technique, as well as a display
of a lack of understanding of the secondary school student.

The lecture has some place in high school social science
classes, in combination with any of the progressive plans
as well as with other older methods, but the lecturing can
easily be overdone. Unless a teacher has exceptional facility and inspiration, the method is a certain threat to
student interest and enthusiasm. Even in college and
university, the persistent droning out of information and
explanations day after day for the entire class period by
uninspired talkers stamps the uneducative medievalism
of our higher institutions as compared with the skilled
craftsmanship of elementary instruction. Such lecturing
had its place only in the early days of the universities
when the art of bookmaking was still far from adequate
in furnishing inexpensive and convenient sources of information. In modern education, even on the higher
levels, the use of the lecture has little justification for
anything but the critical evaluations or distinctive points
of view of academic authorities or the inspirational introduction of new fields of study.

Such uses can and should be found for the lecture in
high school work as well. Extended, full period efforts of
this sort will very rarely be justified. The short, carefully
prepared talk by the teacher to introduce a new unit of
work or to summarize and evaluate a completed one or to
arouse interest in a new problem needs no defense. Such
talks must be clear, interesting, enthusiastic, as well as

brief. Facility in this art should be consciously cultivated by the social science teacher, as certainly as effective dramatic reading must be one of the arts of the English teacher. Such talks should never be continued if the slightest inattention is observed. The teacher who does so shows a striking lack of understanding of his students' tolerance and a sad underestimate of their good judgment. One of the most serious faults of the social studies teachers is this habit of loose, endless talk. There is no surer way in history classes of killing interest or of defeating personal initiative and active mental reaction than the excessive use of the lecture method.

The place of dates and facts.—While the materials and methods in progressive teaching give greater emphasis to the discussion and understanding of problems in American history and government, it is not to be inferred that the thorough learning of important facts is not approved. By eliminating the large mass of scholastic detail so characteristic of the typical high school text, the way may be made clear for the more complete mastery of essentials. There need be no apology for requiring students to memorize as well as understand a selected list of important dates, events, time sequences, outlines of movements, and cause-and-effect relationships.

The extreme modern attitude that disapproves of memorization, reviews, and even drill on a list of important essential facts in the social studies deprives the students of one of the principal permanent values of such work in the schools. Such basic information is necessary for further intelligent reading and for permanent cultural and civic uses. A thorough knowledge of pivotal dates, events, locations, and sequences is the basis for all future orientation in history reading and in political discussions.

In connection with this phase of thorough learning, a few additional suggestions may be given:

1. In the matter of dates and their associated events, take the students into your confidence in a very specific way as to what you expect them to memorize. A list of from fifteen to twenty-five dates in American history should be prepared by the teacher. Such lists are available as the result of a number of research studies that represent widespread evaluations by historians and teachers.

2. The best time to evaluate such lists of required dates is in connection with the discussion of the previews for each unit of work. Cumulative reviews can be given in connection with successive assignments. Broad movements in history may similarly be emphasized to form a factual core for a course.

3. The teacher should realize and should help students understand that the learning of an important factual core is provided for in the cyclical plan of curriculum in most school systems, that a part of the necessary work of a high school course is a review of some essentials learned in the elementary school course, and that a similar relearning in ever-widening circles of association with pivotal facts may be built up in all future reading.

4. A part of the learning experience for such selected minimal essentials should be provided by the teacher's ingenuity in seeing that core materials are actually used in class discussions and in study, especially in reasoning exercises with date-event items and cause-and-effect sequences. The value of such a memorized core of facts should be demonstrated to the students in discussion or study periods by requiring them to reason from such essential basic facts to

related details and by the relation of such facts to larger movements, epochs, and trends.

5. Unless a strict and judicious limitation is placed on such lists of dates and facts, there is serious danger that students will mechanically memorize meaningless masses of words.

The dangers of overemphasis on the factual, informational elements are exceptionally hard to resist in history, in geography, in civics. There are elaborate patterns of fact, mosaics that charm more and more as one specializing in these subjects adds detail upon detail to the designs he has discovered in the relationships of the bits to one another and to the whole. Often the adult, specialized, professional point of view, in teachers as well as in textbook writers, transforms the simple narrative of history or the descriptions of geography and government into logical abstractions of movement, trend, or relationship that have no meaning to the pupil. Massed factual details, and the patterns that organize them for the adult, become meaningless verbal jumbles for the student. The thought loses its reality in a maze of words that have no meaning. The Report of the Commission on the Social Studies of the American Historical Association warns against the dangers of such unintelligent instruction, declaring that ". . . verbalism, the use of words without understanding, has cursed the school all down through the centuries and, as investigations by the Commission prove, continues to corrupt social science instruction in American schools today." [2]

In the same connection the Commission implies the means of substituting reality for such verbalism, by adjusting ". . . instruction to the experience and ability of the pupil in order that the knowledge, powers, and

[2] In *Conclusions and Recommendations*, p. 79.

loyalties acquired will be useful and related to the world in which the pupil actually lives and thinks and acts." [3]

Cautious experimenting with new methods.—This discussion of methods and devices may be concluded with a bit of advice as to the eclectic and experimental use of the new methods that have been described. All teachers owe it to themselves to be progressing in technique as well as growing in a constant mastery of subject matter. The general methods and special devices presented in this book are believed to be the most commendable and most progressive in the experience of successful history and civics teaching. Sufficient variety of technique has been suggested so that the teacher may choose. If any of the plans outlined have not been tried, it is urged that some experimentation in technique be undertaken. A trial of one or two new forms of instruction each year will help to raise the teacher above the dead level of textbook recitation and lecturing. Eclectic innovations in technique will help to vitalize class interest in the social studies courses, just as the teacher's continuous reading in the subjects will help to enrich the course and to inspire interest in our national history and government.

It may not be out of place to offer some advice to teachers who are contemplating the substitution of one of the progressive plans for any of the more traditional methods. In general this advice may be summarized in the caution to make the substitution gradually. This will apply especially to all of the newer methods, with the possible exception of the workbook plan. This may be considered as either a supplement to any of the traditional plans of study and instruction or as a substitute prepared so completely in detail that the caution may not seem necessary.

If a teacher is contemplating the unit plan, some pre-

[3] *Op. cit.,* p. 78.

pared course of study in which this has been worked out in detail should be secured and studied carefully for outlines and methods suggestions. A tentative experiment should then be tried for a single unit before committing oneself to the program for a whole semester.

If the problem method is considered attractive, an occasional lesson based on a current problem should be tried out before a whole semester's work is projected along these lines. Similarly, trials of some of the laboratory or socializing devices may be introduced gradually. Some may be adopted for permanent use, either as variations of one's present plans, or as a basis for a steady expansion and combination of these methods, or as a gradual transition to a new technique.

The integration plan should probably not be adopted outright by any teacher who has not the spirit of an enthusiastic pioneer, or by one who has not acquired considerable confidence by an extended experimentation with methods. It would perhaps be more advisable for most teachers to introduce gradually for a year or two some of the experiments suggested in the two preceding paragraphs and then attempt the integrating program if approval can be secured from principal or department heads.

A gradual, conscientious trial of some of the newer elements will be far more likely to meet with success than a complete substitution of some untried novelty for a habit of method. This is advised, not from a lack of confidence in the newer methods, but in a spirit of practical helpfulness to the teacher.

BIBLIOGRAPHY

Bye, E. C.: *Bibliography on the Teaching of the Social Studies.* New York: H. W. Wilson Company, 1933.

Collings, Ellsworth: *Progressive Teaching in Secondary Schools.* Indianapolis: Bobbs-Merrill Company, 1931.

Crawford, C. C., and McDonald, L. P.: *Modern Methods in*

Teaching Geography. Boston: Houghton Mifflin Company, 1929.

Dawson, Edgar: *Teaching the Social Studies.* New York: The Macmillan Company, 1927, Chapter XIII.

Dewey, Evelyn: *The Dalton Laboratory Plan.* New York: E. P. Dutton & Company, Inc., 1922.

Johnson, Henry: *The Teaching of History in Elementary and Secondary Schools.* New York: The Macmillan Company, 1920, Chapters XI-XIII.

Klapper, Paul: *The Teaching of History.* New York: D. Appleton-Century Company, 1926, Chapters XIV, XV, and XIX.

Knowlton, Daniel C.: *History and the Other Social Studies in the Junior High School.* New York: Charles Scribner's Sons, 1926, Chapter VI.

Tryon, R. M.: *The Teaching of History in Junior and Senior High Schools.* Boston: Ginn & Company, 1921, Chapters I-VII.

PERIODICALS

Rugg, E. U.: "Some Learning Implications in the Social Studies." *Historical Outlook,* December, 1927, pp. 369-373.

CHAPTER VIII

OBJECTIVES IN THE SOCIAL STUDIES

Immediate and ultimate aims.—Preliminary to a discussion of objectives in the social studies it may be advisable to raise the question whether immediate or ultimate aims have been more prominent in determining the curriculum and methods in the social studies. Common practice in this matter should be examined critically to determine whether, in view of recent changes in content and methods, the same general aims may still be valid— whether we shall continue toward the same goals or new ones in teaching history, geography, civics, and related subjects.

When we review the elaborate discussions of objectives that have been made in the past surveys of practices in the schools or in the tabulation of opinions of experts and specialists in the universities and high schools, comparing them with the discussion of aims proposed by the leading advocates of reform, we shall find much less change than might have been anticipated. We find a somewhat stronger emphasis on the importance of some immediate values, but no diminution of the significance of ultimate results. We find an increased insistence on the value of certain study skills for both immediate and ultimate purposes, and a rather extreme negative evaluation of the permanent learning or retention of facts for their own sake or for academic demands. There is also a stronger insistence on the importance of instilling certain permanent attitudes, but these attitudes are the same that have long been considered essential.

In a general way, the aims that have been held as the

177

most important in the teaching of the social studies in the public schools are college preparation, general culture, good citizenship, and certain distinctive study skills. In a general comparison it may be said that the recent movements in the reform of social studies teaching have tended to increase the importance of citizenship and study skills, to advocate slightly less emphasis on college preparation, and to give a new interpretation of culture. In general these changes are involved in the stress placed on attitudes and skills as contrasted with the more traditional emphasis on the acquisition of factual information.

If we may take these four general aims as highly important in the opinion of recent leaders as well as of the more conservative subject specialists, we can readily see that all of these aims, with the possible exception of the college preparatory objective, can and do have both immediate and ultimate possibilities. The preparation for college requirements is a value that lies so near in the student's future that the distinction between immediate and ultimate loses its significance here. But in matters of culture, citizenship, and study technique we have such clearly recognizable values for both the immediate use of the student and for his permanent equipment throughout adult life that it may be worth while to contrast the aims in terms of present and future values.

This contrast may perhaps be made clear by a dogmatic declaration of belief in the transcendent importance of the ultimate, lifelong, cultural interests, civic attitudes, and study skills that should be the product of all school work in all of the social studies. The permanent cultural inspirations and interests are not to be considered inferior even to those of literature and the arts, if indeed one can continue to think of these as distinct from the social studies field. The adult attitudes in civic conduct are not to be recognized as subordinate to any but moral ideals, and only so when the two may seem to conflict. The skills in reading and research that may be trained for lifelong efficiency in the social studies are more comprehensive and practical than can be claimed as inherent in any line of subject matter in the schools. The comparison of abilities for adult use may, in this group of objectives, confidently be compared even with the techniques of literature or science.

In asserting the great ultimate values of work in the social studies there is, however, no intention of slighting their immediate possibilities for the student in his present-day activities and needs. There is rather an implication that, in so far as permanent interests, attitudes, and skills are emphasized in the social studies, we are dealing with objectives that will achieve immediate results as soon as, and to the degree that, they are instilled and cultivated. These ultimate objectives can only be achieved by immediate practice and application.

Distorted emphasis on facts.—It is only when we think of certain common teaching practices that we come to realize the distinction that can be drawn between immediate and ultimate values. When such a distinction is clearly seen, we are driven to the conclusion that lies at the basis of much of the proposed reform in social studies teaching: any material or activity that has only immediate values has no value at all. In this type of work falls much of the study in history, geography, and civics, where blind emphasis is put on the learning of facts for purposes of recitation, testing, or final examinations. This purblind attachment of importance to facts, based on a comparative evaluation of events or processes with which they are connected, is the unfortunate pedagogical evaluation that comes to many teachers of subjects that are richly burdened with factual information.

This unfortunate emphasis on the knowledge element in the social studies classroom, which has usually deteriorated into a memorization exercise on the part of pupils and an informational testing activity on the part of the teacher, not only has brought the criticism of the progressive educational philosopher, but has too often defeated the attainment of the ultimate goals which the social studies teachers of the past had fervently professed and fatuously believed they were attaining. Instead of instilling cultural interests in the rich fields of history, biography, politics, human activity, and natural wonder, they were, by their shortsighted imposition of memorizing tasks, defeating their own ultimate aim. They were permanently destroying the possibility of such interests; they were creating a distaste for all reading in their subjects in the future. In contrast to this ignoring of ultimate effects, the progressive educator advocates a method and a disregard of chronologies, and logic, and subject-minded divisions, on the theory that if the interests and attitudes are achieved, the facts will take care of themselves. He sees in facts merely a means to an end, a vehicle for promoting interests, for practice in study skills, for understanding of relationships and duties, for inspiring attitudes. In the cultural field, where knowledge serves as content, the progressive social science teacher strives to contribute his share to a liberal education by arousing and feeding all the interests we naturally have in our fellow human beings, past and present, remote and near, in groups and as individuals.

The shortsighted policy of evaluating the student's work in the social studies in terms of immediate academic achievement, his performance in recitations and tests and examinations, has been one of the mistakes most directly attacked by those who have championed changes in method, new combinations in content, and a better perspective in objectives. The academic values have been reconstructed as means to other ends, rather than ends in themselves. The subject-minded specialist's point of view has been subordinated to more significant human, social values. The student's present environment in the community, his relations to the community, both now and later, his service to it as well as its influence on him, his equipment for conduct by training in attitudes and skills —all these are being made significant in social studies objectives, rather than his memorizing of facts for the emergencies of tests and the earning of school grades.

Limitations in all testing.—In the social sciences, perhaps more than in any other subject taught in the public schools, results of classroom instruction and experiences cannot be evaluated by such immediate reactions as may be revealed by any form of testing. Whether we use old-type written examinations or the most ingeniously contrived objective tests of the new type, we shall never know if our teaching has been really successful. The social studies teacher has a right to believe in deferred dividends. Qualities, abilities, attitudes, and interests must be produced that can only be judged in the future life of the student. Especially if we have in mind the character and citizenship objectives, do we realize how uncertain we must be about the product of the school. Tests have not been devised that will predict probable future conduct or the application of present skills and interests even in the immediate life outside of school.

The importance of evaluating the content of a subject to determine the essential from the less significant in the realm of facts must be recognized if we are to give special emphasis to the essentials and if we are to apply sensible methods in the thorough learning of such essentials by review and drill. While we are justified in using the study guide for such evaluations and the workbook for thoroughness, as well as the test to determine the student's degree of mastery, we cannot hope to determine or impress the whole effect of such efforts.

This limitation of all testing, as well as the distinction between immediate, factual, testable results and the larger aims of social science instruction have been strikingly expressed in the Report of the Commission on Social Studies of the American Historical Association in the declaration that "The competent teacher, while avoiding all forms of academic pedantry and distinguishing the significant from the trivial, will know that learning is usually a difficult and arduous business, will make provision for indispensable drill and repetition, and will prepare and administer tests of progress from time to time; but in it all he will appraise with appropriate humility the adequacy of his own judgments and of any classroom examinations to measure the long-time social results of instruction." [1]

General aims and specific objectives.—On the basis of the four general aims that have been suggested as acceptable to both the traditional exponents of the social subjects and the progressive leaders in the movements for unified or integrating courses by methods which emphasize pupil needs and interests, it would be possible to draw up elaborate lists of specific objectives. This is not, however, the purpose of this chapter. Rather are we interested in a comparison of general aims and in the directions that specific objectives will take if the new methods and modified content are substituted for the old. In such a comparison we are specially concerned with the change in emphasis that will come over our aims if the spirit of our teaching is made to conform with the progressive philosophy and values of learning experiences in the social studies field.

[1] In *Conclusions and Recommendations*, p. 82.

Most fundamental of all in the changes of emphasis will be the subordination of fact learning to the development of a permanent interest and to the exposure of individual pupils to specific interests, many, various, intense interests, quite regardless of balance, and with a rather frank recognition that not even in high school, not even in college, nor in the most devoted career of adult scholarship, can a thoroughgoing completeness in the mastery of factual detail serve any purpose except the astounding but useless display of uncultured erudition or scholastic futility. The man who never gets a date wrong may be able to correct the proofreader of an encyclopedia, but the effort will make him as useless in civic functioning as a comptometer and as interesting in social intercourse as an abacus.

The process of translating general aims into specific objectives for particular units or activities or lessons has been carried to a staggering degree of detail by state or university curriculum experts and by course of study committees in many of the metropolitan school systems. The reading of such lists may give a teacher an insight into a technique that may often be applied spontaneously to the purposes of a particular lesson or to the emergencies of a special occasion. The formal application of such specific motives to particular units of subject matter is quite inconsistent with the whole spirit of the progressive movement; it is, in fact, hardly complimentary to good teaching even of the formal textbook type. The vision and insight of the teacher can be relied on to make such detailed application of purposes most effectively as the needs of the day or of the individual may dictate.

How objectives should be determined.—The objectives of teaching for any subject in the public schools have in the past been largely determined by a number of different influences and agencies—textbook writers, state, county, and city school administrators, normal schools, and certain determined organized groups sponsoring some special aim. All of these focused quite directly on the teacher, either by particular prescriptions as to the content of courses and textbooks or by direction or appeals to her ideals and attitudes of emphasis. Some of these influences were national, some local; some were direct, others indirect. The common method was to have a body of subject matter prescribed, and it was usually taken for granted that some form of memoriter learning of this material would function as a control of the pupils' future conduct. In short, the whole selection of objectives was largely a matter of individual, subjective incubation and was dished up to the teacher in the shell of subject matter content.

In recent years a more direct and objective determination of the aims of education has been undertaken. The whole process of co-operative research to determine the specific objectives for each subject and for different levels of instruction cannot be given in detail. Two recent statements as to this method may serve adequately to describe its real nature and its superior value as compared to the traditional method of individual guess, administrative fiat, and minority clamor.

Bobbitt has described the method, and tabulated the results in several volumes. His procedure may be summarized in these few sentences:

"When we know what men and women ought to do along the many lines and levels of human experience, then we shall have before us the things for which they should be trained. The first task is to discover the activities which ought to make up the lives of men and women; and along with these, the abilities and personal qualities necessary for proper performance. These are the educational objectives.

"The plan to be employed is activity-analysis. The first step is to analyze the broad range of human experience into major fields. . . .

"The major fields of human action having been defined, the second step is to take them, one after the other, and analyze them into their more specific activities." [2]

The same process and method is urged in the briefer form of "A Golden Rule of Education" by Briggs. "The first duty of the school is to teach pupils to do better the desirable things that they are likely to do anyway." Later he adds that this "needs to be supplemented at least by the following: Another duty of the school is to reveal higher activities and to make them both desired and to a maximum extent possible." [3]

This process of scientific, objective determination has now been going on for a decade or more, by research at the universities, by endowed surveys, by elaborate curriculum committees, or by departments of experts in the larger city school systems. Exhaustive compilations have been published for every subject taught in the public schools, and, in many collections, these have been grouped for each grade level, on the basis of expert judgment, teacher experience, or careful experimentation. The results are now a prominent feature of teacher-training courses, and it may be assumed that teachers are now qualified or can readily inform themselves of the desirable goals that may be kept in mind for the leading activities of each day's work. The immediate selection and application of specific objectives for particular tasks must

[2] Bobbitt, Franklin, *How to Make a Curriculum*. Boston: Houghton Mifflin Company, 1924, pp. 8-9.

[3] Briggs, Thomas H., *Secondary Education*. New York: The Macmillan Company, 1933, pp. 258, 263.

be left to the teacher's judgment. The relation of these to
the occasion, to the individual needs and abilities of students, to the unit or activity in hand must remain as the
responsibility of the classroom teacher. Advice, exposure,
and training in the relation of aims to subject matter and
to teacher activities and pupil experiences are the functions of training-school teachers and of supervisors; the
execution of selection and adaptation, shifting from day
to day, from lesson to lesson, and from one pupil to another is the function of the teacher.

Objectives affected by current conditions.—This freedom of the teacher to adapt objectives to special emergencies may be illustrated in a single phase to demonstrate the principle. The circumstances of current events
bring about a constant shift in interest from one topic
to another. The importance of utilizing the natural vitalizing values of current interests, as well as the convenience of having suitable information available in the
newspapers and magazines, have already been explained
fully in Chapter III. The close relation of certain subject
matter and of particular activities to specific objectives
has also been made clear. When some political event in
Washington holds public attention one week, when this
shifts to some movement in the suppression of crime, and
then to some significant local community enterprise, there
must be as rapid a change from one objective to another
as there is in the events themselves. A Supreme Court decision on an important monetary principle may involve
an objective of mere understanding of an economic problem. A community drive for some welfare movement will
call for participation in a co-operative activity sponsored
by the school. Adjustments to a program of social studies
in such close contact with present real-life situations cannot be planned in advance by supervisors or curriculum
directors. The values of participation in realities that

challenge interest and promise the most effective training can be seized only by the teacher who has been granted freedom of selection and who is willing to subordinate a stereotyped program to the exigencies of real learning. There may be some difficulties in overlapping, some danger of fragmentary contacts, or some violence to subject matter logic, but these will be more than offset by the degree of interest and understanding that comes from immediate use and real experience.

Objectives as related to subjects.—In the past, after each general aim had been analyzed into specific objectives and particular pupil experiences, all these were then classified according to the subjects or fields in which the material was usually presented by the traditional logical divisions. It was sometimes recognized that a particular objective might reasonably be allotted to several subjects, that it was of sufficient importance to warrant a repetition of study experiences in both fields. As the primary step of activity analysis developed into a more and more concrete and practical expression of objectives, the sequences, groupings, and combinations of these objectives began to involve more and more correlation of subject matter in different fields, especially in the solution of current problems, in the carrying out of projects and activities, and in programs of integration. New unities were introduced in this way and some radical reorganizations of the old subjects seemed desirable. The conflict between these new organizations and the logical subjects is certain to continue for some time. Tolerant adjustments and cautious experimentation with combinations of the old and new programs will be in order for a considerable period. Compromises will have to be worked out locally, depending on the extent to which the new types of curriculum organization are adopted. Much of the transitional adjustment will have to be left to the individual teacher.

The same freedom in the selection of materials, regardless of the subjects in which they may conventionally be classified, must be left to the individual teacher in order that subject matter as well as aims may be fitted to individual pupil needs and purposes and to the variations in real-life backgrounds as they emerge in current affairs.

Summary of significant objectives.—Throughout the discussion of the newer methods in the previous chapters it has been suggested that these modifications of teaching procedure had in mind specific objectives in the pupils' experiences and that these objectives could be attained more efficiently by the new techniques than by the more traditional plans. It may be helpful to summarize at this point some of the more important of those aims that have been specially emphasized:

1. To improve the pupil's reading skills, both in rate and comprehension
    a. To make him conscious of his limitations as compared with average standards for his grade
    b. To show him definitely how to improve his skill
    c. To give him confidence in his ability to handle the larger unit reading assignments
2. To make pupils realize the value of getting a broad perspective of a chapter or unit assignment by preliminary rapid survey and skimming
3. To give practice in the comparison of parallel readings and of supplementary materials drawn from different subjects
4. To develop interests in various types of reading material, and in a variety of topics, especially in the fields of biography, travel, and social problems

5. To make a student conscious of, and fairly efficient in, a variety of study methods
   a. How to write a summary sentence for a paragraph
   b. How to summarize a section or chapter
   c. How to outline
   d. How to expand a vocabulary of social science terms by the use of textbooks and reference books and how to practice himself in the use of such terms
   e. How to use a table of contents
   f. How to use an index
   g. How to find answers to questions
   h. How to formulate problems of thought-provoking questions about his reading
   i. How to test himself efficiently with the various objective devices
   j. How to keep alert in social studies reading for cause-and-effect relationships and how to reason these out if they are not fully expressed in the reading assigned
   k. When, where, and how to make use of collateral reading references
   l. An ability to observe intelligently and critically the present-day events in one's community

6. How to read a newspaper efficiently
   a. How to skim headlines and select news worth reading
   b. How to detect and guard against the partisan bias in newspaper editorials, headlines, and stories

7. How to use the leading weekly and monthly news magazines

8. How to use the *Readers' Guide* to find information on any current issue or problem

9. Ability to use such current problems and one's information about them as a source of conversation

10. Ability to evaluate and choose moving-picture entertainment intelligently

11. Ability and desire to select worth-while radio programs

12. Ability to prepare and present effectively a short talk to a group

13. Ability to preside properly at a formal or informal group meeting or discussion

14. Ability to participate graciously and desire to co-operate in such group discussions

15. Ability to participate in the work of a committee as chairman or member

16. Desire to co-operate with fellow-students, teachers, and administrators as a good school citizen

17. Willingness to promote community enterprises by participating in such ways as are adapted to one's abilities

18. Ability to use a school and public library independently
    a. To use card catalogue
    b. To find books
    c. To use all tools of reference

19. Interest in all accessible museums and art galleries

20. Ability to write correctly and with some interest and force one's information and opinions on problems of community and civic importance

21. An understanding of vocational possibilities after leaving school, with interest in several lines of work

22. A conscious program of several worth-while leisure time enterprises, including, at least
    a. One construction activity
    b. A select line of non-fiction reading
    c. Historical and civic curiosity
23. To improve the student's understanding of those distinctive terms in the social studies vocabulary which are important for the clear comprehension of current reading and discussions in the field of civic and social events and theories

Motivation of interest an immediate objective.—The study of all social sciences in the high school should look forward primarily to the building up of permanent interests that will control the pupil's reading throughout life, both for cultural and practical values. The acquaintance with historical facts that will prove of any permanent value must cover a range of reading far beyond the time available in the courses taken in school. The contact with historical persons and problems must be a continuous and progressive affair throughout life. The mere introductory outline and first contact in the typical school course need constant refreshment and enlargement. Studies in human nature, contact with inspiring personalities, and understanding of the important civic and political problems of our nation in the past should be introduced in such a way as to stimulate the interest and imagination of pupils permanently.

Contact with historical facts is a necessary background for all reading in literature, philosophy, and the arts and sciences. This motive may be considered adequate for all social studies courses in the high school, whether we expect the student to make a practical use in civic life of such informational reading or not. Even if we think of history reading as purely a matter of entertainment and recreation, like the reading of fiction, the inspiration for such reading in the school course will be an adequate justification for all time and effort expended. The idle curiosity about how people have lived in our country in the past, the romance of their struggles against material difficulties and their solution of political problems, or similar information about people in other lands and other times, all open a field in the study of human nature that will challenge in richness the imaginary experiences of fictional characters.

Yet the contact with such facts must not become an occasion for academic cramming and memorizing, if such learning serves no other apparent purpose to the student than his performance of an academic task. When the facts have served their purpose of clarifying understanding, arousing interests and sympathies, or building and fortifying attitudes, we need not be greatly concerned if they are forgotten beyond recall, even for the emergencies of testing.

It will be worth while, further, to make a distinction between a general interest in history reading and specific interests for individual students. Both are included, and both are important in connection with this objective. General interest in any sort of historical material is something we have a right to expect in any normal individual. Such reading combines both the narrative and the human interests, the most universal and most intense factors in any person's reading selections. Why history materials, combining these universal interest factors with both romance and realism that rival the most thrilling fiction, should become distasteful by school contact presents a challenge to our objectives and methods of instruction that we cannot ignore. If a pupil should gain a world of fact and yet lose his interest in history reading, we shall have done him more harm than good.

As for specific interests, history is as full of variety as any field, not excluding fictional literature. A general love of biographical reading may here be individualized for particular students in one or more of the outstanding personalities of our country's past. Likewise the history of particular periods or of particular problems presents a variety of goals that are available for any teacher with any class. To sacrifice these possibilities of interest, specialized and individual, for the sake of a more thorough retention of a balanced distribution of factual detail is a most shortsighted confusion of objectives.

Perhaps these specific interests may seem more significant than the general interest in history reading. Possibly the general interest may be best achieved ultimately by a primary appeal to specific interests. Probably the specific interests in problems may be best approached by the primary appeal to an interest in personalities.

This motive of building a permanent interest in the social studies is emphasized as an essential objective by the Commission on the Social Studies of the American Historical Association in its recent report. The Commission declares that "The competent teacher will relate the educative process to the interests of the pupil, not because of any romantic faith in child nature or of any equally romantic distrust of adult society, but rather because learning, in order to be vital, must enlist the active and sustained interest of the learner. At the same time the competent teacher will be constantly aware of the fact that countless interests lie dormant in every child, waiting to be aroused by appropriate experiences, and that he is under professional obligation to develop in the pupil a continuing interest in social affairs." [4]

College entrance examinations and requirements.—In most states the courses in American history and civics are

[4] *Op. cit.,* pp. 80-81.

accepted for entrance credits at the universities and colleges. One or more units in these subjects are generally required for entrance. In this regard, individual colleges and universities are more or less uniformly regulated by the Associations of Colleges and Secondary Schools. In fulfilling this entrance requirement, especially in preparing students for those colleges and universities where entrance examinations are given instead of accepting the student's high school work by accrediting, the teacher is often at a loss as to proper standards of achievement for her classes. Content of a course can be described in terms of textbooks or topical outlines, but quality of work that is satisfactory must be estimated by indirect means.

In the field of the social studies the teacher is not aided as definitely by standardized tests as in some other subjects. The objective tests available in the market represent a very inadequate evaluation of the qualities and range of information and understanding expected for college entrance examinations.

Entrance examinations are still required in the New England and Middle States and are prepared for all institutions in this section of the country by a central board. Definite ideas of the sort of preparation expected can be secured from copies of such examinations given during previous years. It would be advisable for teachers who have a number of students preparing for entrance to eastern colleges to collect and keep a file of such annual examination questions. These will give a definite indication, not only of the topics and problems most frequently emphasized, but also of the nature and thoroughness of the preparation expected.

Whether the teacher is obliged to prepare students for such examinations or not, these entrance requirements are the most reliable index we have of what should be a suitable expectation as to standard of work in all high school history teaching, even for students who are going to universities where their credits will be accepted in the subject without examination. This college preparatory objective may properly be considered as one of the important aims for the high school course. Usually this aim is prominent enough, if not actually overemphasized because of state university pressure. The interest and civic aims should never be sacrificed to this preparatory purpose in high school courses. Such subordination is likely to result in too great an emphasis on factual detail.

It is not only the expectation but the example of the history departments of colleges and universities throughout the country, especially in their undergraduate courses, that is largely responsible for this exaggerated emphasis on factual material in the high schools. History majors, made scholastic in their concepts of social science study and teaching, repeat the knowledge emphasizing rote and cramming methods in which they were molded in college. Many even carry the medieval lecture method of fact teaching into senior and junior high school. The progressive reformation of their method and objectives has largely crept upon them in the form of a rear attack from the changes that have come in from the activity and allied movements in the elementary schools, as well as from the direct assaults of a new educational philosophy that is trying to rescue the pupil from the subject-minded specialist.

In college courses in the social science subjects there are two alleviating circumstances that are probably responsible for a persistence of the natural interest of the young college adult in these fields. One is the expert, often original, interpretations of facts by the abler college lecturer; the other is the requirement of collateral reading in any course in such masses as to permit or compel a wholesome superficiality and a variety of contacts, stimulating an understanding and reflection that results from the comparison of conflicting points of view and interpretations.

In connection with the aim of preparing students for college it must be kept in mind that where the preparation is not for specific entrance examinations, the high school experience in history is under very little handicap as far as progressive ideals and methods of teaching are concerned. Unless students are headed for those eastern schools where entrance examinations are still required, the real preparation for college work in the social studies may be quite free from the incubus of factual cramming in specific divisions of history. In all cases where students are received by the certification of units the ideal preparation for further specialization in the social studies can be directed to the same goals of cultural interests and civic attitudes that have been urged as the ultimate permanent objectives for the social science field. No more helpful preparation for effective majoring in history, political science, or economics in college could be given any student than the inspiration of the interests and attitudes that have been described.

General approval of civic aims.—There is perhaps no general objective in any school work that is so universally understood or so generally accepted with approval as the good citizenship aim in connection with the subjects of American history and civics. It is not only approved by teachers and administrators, but by parents as well. It may even be claimed that the goal of these studies is more clear and acceptable to pupils in both elementary and high school than the purposes of any other learning required of them. In making such a claim it is not necessarily implied that this consciousness of a civic motive involves a realization of all the broader and worthier elements of good citizenship. In fact, in most cases, with teachers and school officials no less than with parents and pupils, the concept is too narrow and nationalistic. But this does not disparage the fact that the belief exists that the social studies are intended and are able to serve a social purpose.

With this thought in mind it may be interesting to examine one of the most recent digests of objectives in the social studies. The figures in the table on page 198 show the relative frequency with which different objectives were mentioned in the social studies courses in sixty important high school centers.

In a glance at the compilation of objectives in this table, it seems clear enough that a large number of the items are merely alternative expressions for the good citizenship aim, or at least that they are obvious logical phases of this important general purpose. Of the twenty-eight captions in the list, at least eleven are directly related to some sort of civic motive, namely, items 1, 2, 3, 5, 7, 9, 10, 11, 13, 14, and 23. Several others are stated in such general or indefinite terms that these also might reasonably be accepted as elements of training for citizenship, items 4, 8, 15, 17, 19, and 22.

To get an understanding of the importance of this good citizenship objective in school work we should make some examination of the spirit in which this is commonly expressed, compare the change in emphasis as the pupil passes from the elementary to the high school, and consider the broader, more inclusive, and worthier concept that has been given this aim in the progressive courses as compared with the older, traditional ideal.

The patriotic and international objectives.—In the past the patriotic objective has been more emphasized than any other as a motive for requiring or encouraging stu-

GENERAL OBJECTIVES LISTED IN SIXTY SOCIAL STUDIES
COURSES REARRANGED FROM SWINDLER'S STUDY [5]

Objectives	Number
1. Socio-civic efficiency	176
2. Participation in civic activities	127
3. Information as a basis for participation	116
4. Making the world intelligible for pupils	114
5. Knowledge of civic rights, duties, and responsibilities	112
6. Ability to think, discriminate, judge	104
7. Knowledge of social, economic, and political principles	93
8. Knowledge of the past in order to interpret the present	87
9. Intelligent patriotism	85
10. Service and co-operation in society	83
11. Respect for law and institutions	74
12. Knowledge of moral, ethical, and religious principles	71
13. Appreciation of the interdependence of nations	63
14. Understanding of the principles of the Constitution and democracy	61
15. Proper attitudes and interests	60
16. Worthy use of leisure	53
17. Tolerance and open-mindedness	44
18. Broadening interests and sympathies	44
19. Orderly development for a static world	41
20. Vocational efficiency	40
21. Mastery of tools and skills	34
22. Understanding of the influences of environment	28
23. Awareness of the meaning of living together in organized society	28
24. General culture	27
25. Cultivation of an interest in reading the social studies for pleasure	25
26. Health and efficiency	25
27. Appreciation of historical and scientific methods	18
28. Worthy home membership	15

dents to take any courses in history or civics. If this phase
of the citizenship motive is stressed too strongly, the
courses in the high school will rise very little above the
level of the typical courses in the elementary schools.
The patriotic aim in the American history teaching in
the grades is acceptable. In the more advanced courses in
the high school the civic motive must be put on a dif-

[5] Swindler, R. E., *Objectives in the Social Studies.* From an unpub-
lished study quoted in Kimmel, W. G., *Instruction in the Social Studies,*
Monograph 17, National Survey of Secondary Education, pp. 6-7.

ferent plane. Instead of blind hero worship and the thoughtless belief in the perfection of our political institutions, the student must now get a balanced understanding of debatable solutions and compromises, of expediency, and of the faltering progress toward democracy and justice in our national evolution.

Unquestioning nationalism must now be tempered by a wider, human point of view. Dangers resulting from a jingoistic patriotism make essential a corrective explanation and understanding of international relations, especially in these days since the World War, when our country has been brought into contact with European and Asiatic affairs in spite of a strong tradition and agitation for maintaining isolation.

The extent to which narrowly patriotic motives still dominate our teaching of the social studies is not revealed by such a tabulation of objectives as is shown in the table based on Swindler's study. The fact that socio-civic efficiency is mentioned twice as often as an objective in these sixty courses as patriotism is no indication of common practice throughout the country. It must not be overlooked that these sixty courses of study represent the more progressive school systems only; the great majority of teachers are still working in schools where the consciousness of a need of curriculum revision, of the effort to formulate objectives, has not yet penetrated. Such teachers are still working with the perspectives of tradition or are still dominated by the conventional aims of textbook makers.

Broader civic objectives.—What should more advanced students of the social studies gain in the line of civic equipment beyond their national pride and devotion to the ideals and achievements of the great leaders of democracy? Above all, an understanding of the mechanism of citizenship, of the needs for further progress, and of the part the individual citizen can and should take in promoting that progress with the agencies we have, and in addition a critical interest in the improvement of those agencies. This period of experience should be, as far as instruction can control it, an introduction to the understanding of present-day civic and political problems, a training in methods of socio-civic study and investigation, and a challenge to the formulation of attitudes and an acceptance of specific responsibilities.

The civic purpose, the training in citizenship, both present and prospective, is properly set as a special function of the social sciences. The recent Report of the Commission on the Social Studies of the American Historical Association urges teachers to recognize the "special responsibilities of the social sciences in leading boys and girls to a fuller understanding and a more effective participation in the complex and dynamic social world of material things, persons, institutions, conflicts, thought, ideals, and aspirations." [6]

This aim is to be kept in mind by teachers of these subjects in order that they may help students achieve "the broad purpose of American education." The realization of this aim involves both understanding and participation—citizenship must be dynamic as well as intelligent.

Should propaganda be an objective?—In social studies one of the problems about aims that is rapidly taking on the semblance of controversy at the present time is whether the school may or should be used to propagate social, political, and economic points of view. In times of change and adjustment, when partisan spirit runs high, and when new political theories and economic remedies are spawned prolifically, champions of every cause insist that the teachers shall become their spokesmen to the younger generation. As these propagandists invade the

[6] In *Conclusions and Recommendations*, p. 78.

schools they are crowded by their opponents. Conservatives and radicals insist alike that they, and they alone, have the right to have their views presented in the institution that is supported by public funds.

What are the embarrassed administrator and the bewildered teacher to do, especially in the social studies, where questions of great political and economic significance find their natural setting? Is it their duty to tell students what to think, as well as teach them how to think, or to expose them to the information and background on which individual judgments and decisions can be based?

Indoctrination as an objective in the social studies is demanded by some educational leaders; it is denounced by others. Some are double-minded about such aims—they approve propaganda in one direction, and deplore it in another. The promotion of theories, the support of institutions, loyalty to all law and to the present Constitution of our government are all involved in the controversy. Some would draw a line at one level or another; some would include or exclude freedom on all sorts of questions. The evil effects of centrally controlled propaganda for the maintenance and strengthening of the government in power are argued by citing the imperial policies of pre-war Germany or present-day Italy and Russia. The argument for freedom in teaching in the public schools as well as the universities is largely based on our Constitutional ideals and our traditional habit of political tolerance.

Under present conditions, with acute problems of governmental evolution in difficult economic circumstances, with unrest and radical changes hostile to democracy in all the world about us, the leading and control of youthful citizenship becomes a keener issue. Along with this there is a realization among those interested, both among the defenders of the *status quo* and the propagandists of reform, that training of future citizenship in the schools no longer consists of a formal exposure to memories of past glories and patriotic heroics. All such interested leaders of adult political thinking demand the co-operation of the teacher, and insist that indoctrination, of their particular ideas, must be made a leading objective of all teachers concerned with the social studies.

If we insist on the teacher's Constitutional rights of freedom of speech, we may still raise the question of his rights as a citizen and his privileges as a teacher. We may offer an answer that is purely idealistic, in terms of the American tradition, or we may raise the issue of the practical advisability of such freedom in a situation affecting a teacher and his students. The teacher who will insist on his full rights of freedom in such a situation must recognize that these rights are inherent in the democratic ideals of government and he can hardly claim consistency if he should use such rights to subvert such a plan of government, whether his personal leanings might incline toward either a Fascist or a Communist extreme in political and economic theory. The problem of rights and duties, with reference to political indoctrination, would be as much a question of professional conscience, whether the propaganda came as a matter of official prescription, or from dictation by influential groups or persons, or whether the ideas arose from the teacher's own thoughtful decisions.

The attitude suggested here may be summarized in a few direct dogmatic statements:

1. The teacher of social studies has no right to propagate opinions subversive to our present Constitutions, national or state. He has the right, and the duty as well, to promote progress in government,

to meet changing conditions and new problems, by the orderly method of amendment provided by our basic instruments of government.

2. The teacher of the social studies should make it one of his citizenship objectives to see that students are informed on arguments pro and con with reference to such vital problems as arise in current thought or that can be intelligently anticipated in the immediate future, in that period when those now in the high school may be expected to be directly involved in the solutions.

3. The teacher of the social studies has no right to accept as objectives the propaganda of those who would use the schools for the promotion of their theories.

4. With reference to the teacher's own ideals in the field of social science problems, he will do well to express his objectives in terms of student research and reflection and individual decision rather than in the direct indoctrinating promotion of such ideas or opinions.

Emphasizing social attitudes as objectives.—Progressive teachers of the social studies are beginning to abandon their subject-mindedness for a strong civic and social idealism. The most helpful specific objectives may best be expressed in a suggestive list of some of the important attitudes to be developed in students in the matter of social relationships. These will include the simpler individual contacts in home, school, and neighborhood as well as the broader connections with the community, state, and nation. Training in such attitudes, determined as they are by social science information, problems, theories, and ideals, has been in mind in all preceding chapters dealing with the newer methods.

A summary list of some of the typical, important social attitudes, with brief explanatory comment, will be in place as a core for a list of specific objectives for the social studies classes.

(1) The attitude of pride in upright character: Every student of junior or senior high school age must get the clear conception that almost every action may contribute either to the welfare or the detriment of the group. He is now intelligent and mature enough to realize that either the disturbing or the helpful type of conduct can attract attention and even gain admiration or approval from some people. The school, and especially the information and experiences of social studies classes, must contribute to building an attitude or habit of always choosing the socially desirable course of action.

The student is now old enough to know that he may choose uprightness, or the socially helpful type of conduct, from various motives—from fear of consequences for hostile attitudes, from a habit of blind unquestioning obedience to authority, from a calculated consciousness of benefit or profit. But the most desirable result will be to have youth realize that the only reliably effective motivation involves a proud, self-reliant choice of such conduct as intelligence and reflection dictate, and an adherence to it in spite of temptation or opposition, in spite of criticism or ridicule, in defiance of personal disadvantage or even serious loss or danger.

The high school student has already learned that in modern life he is thrown into difficult situations, away from any restraining influences of teachers or parents. He must be ready promptly to refuse participation in any conduct of immoral or evil trend. His decision must come, not from memories of precepts or fear of consequences, but from an intelligent and free conviction of virtue. He must learn that he is personally responsible for his own decisions and actions, that his emotions may often conflict with his judgments, and that often he will have to defend his own choice and resist the attitude of other individuals or even of his whole group. He must, however, be able to recognize the true from the false and to feel pride in a firm stand for the true.

This attitude of pride in his own integrity of character then becomes the basic key to the promotion of certain desirable moral attitudes.

A broader and more vital conception of the school's obligation for training in character and personality attitudes will lead us to recognize exceptional opportunities to be utilized incidentally against the background of the social studies in various class discussions and activities. With students at either the junior or senior high school age teachers may feel that they are dealing with the last opportunity to influence permanently their students' attitudes in such important matters as work, recreation, home relations, and reverence.

There must be developed in high school students the concept that any productive work is a service to society and that as such it has dignity and worth. Vocational guidance must help students to select only such an occupation as yields personal enjoyment, pride and satisfaction in the work itself; to realize that there is such an occupation for everyone, and that this compatibility of work and worker is entirely personal. On the contrary, students should be urged never to enter or persist in any type of work which does not give this individual satisfaction. They should be made aware of the importance of free personal choice of their own vocation—to take advice from any, but dictation from none, not even from parents.

Students must also be taught to realize definitely the difference between amusement and recreation, that the spending of money is not necessary to achieve the greatest satisfactions in the enjoyment of leisure. This concept may be forged into a well-tempered attitude in the social science classroom if the teacher will emphasize from time to time those recreational activities that cost little or nothing. The reading of good books, conversation with friends, hiking, thinking and dreaming, playing with children, outdoor games, browsing in libraries, listening to radio broadcasts of plays and music—all of these and many like them are available to all as substitutes for commercialized amusements. The attitude of enjoyment of these true recreations involves the progressive training and nurture of aesthetic appreciations and tastes.

An attitude of respect for home life and its various relationships has a definite and natural setting in classes dealing with the social sciences. Such unfavorable environments as parental neglect, broken homes, the indifferent wealthy parent or the neglectful, ignorant one bring this responsibility to the schools. The child must be given to realize that his home with all its close relationships is worthy of his most fundamental love and respect. With this, too, another set of ideals may be implanted in his consciousness, looking forward to the time when he himself will establish a home. This involves the attitude of respect for the opposite sex and may lead into discussions aimed to set standards in both the hygiene and ethics of sex relations. Idealized concepts of knightly chivalry or of old-fashioned courtesy find an easy setting in much of the social studies material.

The attitudes of respect and reverence can be constantly emphasized in much of the social studies material. Readings in history and literature furnish the richest background to teach indirectly but effectively the application of these ideals to everyday deportment. Perhaps the most important attitude to mold into the lives of young people is reverence for age, authority, office, achievement, heroism, service, character. To these may be added in occasional contexts, if sectarian restriction is not too active, the inspirational values of basic religious concepts. The comforts and conveniences achieved by the intelligence and persistence of inventors and scientists, and the sacrifices to gain tolerance, justice, and democracy by great humanitarian leaders fill the pages of history with models, heroes, and movements that command respect or inspire reverence.

All these specific phases of ethical conduct are but illustrations of the wealth of material that can be used to give concrete embodiment to the problem of school training in character, and that may be made the subject of conscious pride in self-reliant motivation.

(2) The attitude of co-operation in a group: In addition to the moral relationships which have been defined in terms of social or group welfare, there are a number of group relationships which may be thought of as attitudes of working technique rather than moral ends. These techniques of co-operative relationship the high school student should also develop by his school experiences so that their application to after-school situations may be expected as a matter of social habit.

Any classroom situation is nearly enough analogous to any adult group so that it may be used for the promotion of experiences that will teach each student the methods and attitudes important for successful participation in group activity, whether this success is to be measured in terms of group welfare or of individual advantage.

The student must get the attitude of conforming to the will of the majority as a general rule. He must, on the contrary, also learn to assert his moral integrity against domination by the majority where he has honest doubts about the propriety of its decision. He must learn to initiate machinery to influence the activity of the group. He must get the urge to offer himself generously for group welfare. He must learn to overcome fears and inhibitions and equally must he learn the modesty that will avoid "grandstand" displays to attract attention. He must learn not to pout or balk when defeated. He must learn the technique of teamwork in committees or in minorities, either to promote or to make orderly resistance to parliamentary procedures. He must, therefore, recognize the distinction between a formally organized group and the unorganized, inchoate collection of individuals that still have group possibilities because of common needs.

(3) The attitude of respect for the convictions of others: Students in high school are apt to reflect the opinions and convictions of their homes with reference to a number of social, economic, and political problems. These reflections of home heritage are likely to represent all shades of religious, partisan, and class belief. In no phase of school work is there so much occasion to correct and direct student attitudes of respect and tolerance for the convictions of others as in the social studies classes. The task is a difficult one, but youth especially must learn that everyone has the right to hold and express a different or even a wrong opinion, no matter how erratic, how radical, or how reactionary it may be. If such beliefs or points of view are expressed in class discussions, students should be trained to realize that if they consider a change of belief desirable in others, it should be attempted only by the most tactful and kindly argument, by calm reasoning, never by heated contradiction or scoffing ridicule. Youth must learn that others have the right to maintain their convictions even though they may not be able to defend them. Students should be made conscious of how ugly and rude are dogmatic, intolerant attitudes, or per-

sistent proselyting, or the priggish insistence on the superior merit of one's own opinions.

(4) An attitude of challenge in reading: The best students are often the most docile mentally. It is decidedly desirable to protect these best readers against an easy acceptance of printed opinion. Printer's ink tends to invest opinion with the glamor and authority of truth for most people. The difference between truth and error, fact and opinion, is lost to many on the printed page. Willful misstatement, subtle misinterpretation of facts, purposeful distortion by selective emphasis are devices which the high school student is mature enough to be warned and trained to challenge. The practice of challenge and of reasonable questioning should be cultivated until it becomes an habitual attitude. For practice in this challenging attitude the social studies present a wealth of material for judicious comparisons of conflicting accounts and of disagreeing authorities.

(5) An attitude of active participation in community affairs: Both the classroom and the school as a whole give an opportunity for students to begin the practice and to acquire the sense of obligation to participate in the activities of the community. The ideal of civic service can and should be developed beyond the stage of mere willing performance of responsibilities imposed. There must be a conscious desire to take the initiative in promoting enterprises for the welfare of the group. The school, with its many extracurricular activities, presents a natural situation for training in this important civic attitude. An approach to this training for the larger community activities may be found in many of the situations that have been suggested for the social science classroom in the preceding chapters.

(6) An attitude of active citizenship: The specific political activities may give an even more direct and

practical element of purpose to the particular materials of history and civics than the broader social contacts of community life that have just been discussed. The duties of suffrage and the attitudes students should take in this matter when they become voters can be taught both in theory and practice in the junior and senior high school. Classroom organization and the extracurricular activities of the school present to the progressive teacher an excellent training ground for the development of correct attitudes toward suffrage. School and class elections should be discussed freely in civics classes to create in the minds of students principles and standards of evaluating both the efficiency and character of those they choose as leaders and representatives. Analogous discussions of local, state, and national elections, for vicarious practice in the technique of getting information about candidates, should be introduced into social science classes. Candidates for public office, platforms, publicity, and partisan propaganda, initiative and referendum measures should be laid before students for serious investigation as a training in the thoughtful deliberation about the preliminaries of intelligent voting. Famous elections of the past, with an analysis of emotional, sectional, and partisan factors involved, may be used to point the need for an attitude of intelligent exercise of suffrage responsibilities.

(7) A conscientious attitude with respect to obedience to law: Students being trained for active citizenship should be made to understand that in a representative democracy most laws are the result of compromise between conflicting political groups, a majority and one or several minorities. Often no faction is fully satisfied with the final result. Even when one party dominates by large numbers in either state or nation, cliques or blocs within the party, with different sectional attitudes and desires,

often make a partisan law a compromise. Youth's intolerance of compromise and its impatience with dictation of authority or majority make the problem of obedience or revolt a serious one for training in attitude.

Basically an attitude of respect for law and obedience to the will of the majority must be the first step in civic training. This general principle of conduct must be instilled first; the rare exception of conflict to preserve one's integrity of character may be considered as a later corollary. Students should learn in their classwork and school activities the necessity of orderly, parliamentary procedure, and the general acceptance of majority rule. Disorder, violence, and disobedience should have no place in their school relations. Students should be taught to obey and respect undesirable laws passed by the group until they, by their own open, legal opposition, can gain enough strength to change them by regular procedure. If this be impossible, they should be taught to accept the results of defeat.

In rare instances this may involve the moral conflict of individual integrity against social domination, of the sacrifice of character to the demands of social compromise. In school life or real life such a problem of attitude and conduct is a vital one that may be raised by the student. If the law in question is one that is absolutely opposed to some moral scrupple that the individual has always held sacred, the problem of conscientious objection or disobedience, of opposition by non-co-operation, which has been made conspicuous in real life by recent defiant martyrdoms in world crises, may be raised. Whether such an issue arises in practical situations or in theoretical discussions that are intended to mold student attitudes, the teacher must emphasize not only the seriousness of such decisions for both the individual and society, but the fact that the antisocial attitude can be justified only after the most searching analysis and reflection, that such decisions to disobey the will of the group cannot be made on whim or impulse. It should also be understood that society has the right to punish such defiance of its expressed will and that such punishment must be risked and accepted in the spirit of martyrdom for a moral cause.

(8) An attitude of intent to continue education .throughout life: The determination to continue a self-initiated education beyond the period of school requirements in the fields of vocation, citizenship, and culture should be considered the most natural outcome of school days. How often the school fails to achieve this inspiration! The spirit of antagonism toward learning, which is often aroused, offers a serious condemnation of our method. As the school's permanent endowment of its students, this emotionalized curiosity for more and more learning, this varied and vital interest in continued reading and study, is far more significant than actual learning attainments. When we realize how simply this permanent legacy of purpose may be passed on, it seems strange that so few teachers should achieve it. A single word at the right moment, a directed encouragement in interested research, the brief, luring synopsis of an inspirational book may consciously or unconsciously change the entire intellectual and aesthetic future of a child. Enthusiastic contagion in the vocational or avocational interests of a student may be the spark to fire the imagination and efforts of youth. Even those of average ability, who are beginning to feel that the requirements of college are going to be out of the question for their limitations, can and should be led to realize and desire the possibilities of mental progress through all their days even though the career of formal learning may be closed to them.

BIBLIOGRAPHY

American Historical Association: *Conclusions and Recommendations of the Commission on the Social Studies.* New York: Charles Scribner's Sons, 1934.

Beard, C. A.: *A Charter for the Social Sciences in the Schools.* (Part I of the Report of the American Historical Association Commission on the Social Studies.) New York: Charles Scribner's Sons, 1932.

Beard, C. A.: *The Nature of the Social Sciences in Relation to the Objectives of Instruction.* New York: Charles Scribner's Sons, 1934.

Bobbitt, Franklin: *The Curriculum.* Boston: Houghton Mifflin Company, 1918.

—— *How to Make a Curriculum.* Boston: Houghton Mifflin Company, 1924, Chapters II, VI, VII, and XVI.

Briggs, T. H.: *Secondary Education.* New York: The Macmillan Company, 1933, Chapters XVIII to XXVII.

Charters, W. W.: *The Teaching of Ideals.* New York: The Macmillan Company, 1927.

College Entrance Board: *Examination Questions.* Boston: Ginn & Company.

Dawson, Edgar: *Teaching the Social Studies.* New York: The Macmillan Company, 1927, Chapters XI and XII.

Hockett, John A.: *Determination of the Major Social Problems of American Life.* New York: Bureau of Publications, Teachers College, Columbia University, 1927.

Johnson, Henry: *The Teaching of History in Elementary and Secondary Schools.* New York: The Macmillan Company, 1915.

Klapper, Paul: *The Teaching of History.* New York: D. Appleton-Century Company, 1926, Chapters II, IV, and X.

Morrison, H. C.: *The Practice of Teaching in the Secondary School.* Chicago: University of Chicago Press, 1926.

Peters, C. C.: *Objectives and Procedures in Civic Education.* New York: Longmans, Green & Company, 1930.

Snedden, David: *Sociological Determination of the Objectives of Education*. Philadelphia: J. P. Lippincott Company, 1921.

Tryon, R. M.: *The Teaching of History in Junior and Senior High Schools*. Boston: Ginn & Company, 1921.

Periodicals

Snedden, David: "Social Studies for What?" *School and Society*, September 17, 1932, pp. 358-362.

INDEX

Dalton plan, 28, 42
Dark room, in social studies laboratory, 113
Darrow, Ben. H., 75
Date charts, unit-plan activity, 18
Date lists, 171
Dates and facts, place of, 171-174
Dates, book of, 112
Dawson, Edgar, 119, 176, 213
Debates, unit-plan activity, 18
De Garmo, Charles, 22
Denver, unit plans in, 8
Departmentalization, evils of, 22
Dewey, Evelyn, 176
Dewey, John, 75; new philosophy of education, 157; on integration, 154
Diagnosis, by workbooks, 34
Diaries, imaginary, 115; unit-plan activity, 18
Dictionary, 105; in social studies laboratory, 112; use of, 167
Discussion, conditions for socialized, 90; in unit plan, 12-13; with open textbooks, 165-167
Double period for integration, 122
Dramatization, 114, 115; in laboratory method, 98; unit-plan activity, 17
Drawing boards, in social studies laboratory, 112
Drawing, freehand, 112; mechanical, 112
Drill in social studies, 33-34; supplementary, in workbooks, 32-33

Eclectic innovations, 174-175
Education for life, 212 f.
Elston, B., 119
Encyclopedia, 105; in social studies laboratory, 112; for social studies, 110
English activities in integrated courses, 128-131
English, content values of, 143-144; dangers to, in high school, 150; instrumental use of, 143; integrated with social studies, 120-156; on social studies background, 125-127; requirements

in, dictated by college, 146; teachers of, objections to integration, 149-150
English Round Table, on free reading, 146
Equipment for laboratory work, 111-114
Essays, in laboratory work, 115
Ethical conduct, 207
Exhibits, unit-plan activity, 18
Experimentation with new methods, 174-175
Expression motive in activities, 18-19

Fact learning, subordination of, 183; not an objective, 177
Facts and dates, place of, 171-174; distorted emphasis on, 179-181; requirements of, 196
Fancler, D. G., 75, 96
Fascism, 202
Field trips, 116-117; in laboratory method, 98; unit-plan activity, 17
Filing case, in social studies laboratory, 113
Films, 115
First-aid equipment, in social studies laboratory, 113
Folk songs in social studies laboratory, 113
Forum, The, problem-method source, 64
Free reading, 145, 146-148; unit-plan activity, 17
Freeman, F. N., 76
Frontier in politics, unit plan based on, 6
Fusion (see Integration)
Fusion classes, administration of, 123-125
Fusion courses, 123; extreme forms of, 151-155; of social studies, 26

Galleries, visits to, 117
Gambrill, J. M., 26
German schools under the Republic, 116
Gestalt psychology, 153

Date Due